CONTENTS

PREFACE

In writing *Spiral Ceiling*, I took a journey back in time. Like most such trips, it was a voyage of discovery and a source of both pride and shame. When I embarked, the wind in my sails was long-suppressed anger. The anger came from a secret conviction that I never achieved what I had envisioned. I thought I could have been one of the missing female science professors at Harvard, if not for the roadblocks I'd encountered. I thought I had the potential to make major scientific discoveries such as the translation of the genetic code, and should have risen to the top of my field. What I remembered of my goals turned out not to match what I reconstructed during my writing. By the time I completed this book, I was riding on a strong, fresh wind of joy that I had achieved a balanced life, never having to give up my quest to unveil the unknown. I saw times and places in my life where my progress took a new compass point based on what I always wanted: both to have a family and a realistic chance to discover the hidden logic of genes. When I compared my end point with that of women who strictly pursued science, I was glad to be where I arrived in time and space.

On this writing journey, I had to use fragments of evidence to evoke my past life. Photographs were surprisingly effective in taking me back into moments long ago. At other times, I simply gazed at my garden and tried to move through time to the period I was considering, using whatever cues I could. My friend, Beverly, said, "You must have had extensive notes to be able to use so much conversation." I have an ear for dialogue, but I am sure that frequently the words in this book are not the exact words spoken. I tried my best to capture the flavor and emotions of the conversations. When I visit the past, I "hear" dialogue in my mind.

I have often shown chapters on particular times to my friends, who may recall what happened better than I do. I am particularly interested in their sense of whether quotations from them sound "wrong," so I can quote them correctly. They almost never say that, but more frequently they respond, "I did say something like that, but you didn't completely understand." They then explain what I wish I had realized in the past. What they tell me is enormously interesting, but this book is about how my understanding of myself as a woman in science changed over time. I cannot incorporate those retrospective insights and still fairly represent my own progress. *Spiral Ceiling* is, and must be, based on my own memory of the events, not what others felt.

The resulting memoir is what I wanted desperately in college—a book depicting a woman immersed in both first-class science and warm human relationships. I have succeeded; that insight is my reward for writing this book. At various turning points, I selected a both-family-and-science pathway over my other choices. For my readers, I hope your reward is the realization that "having it all," balancing family relationships with career, is indeed possible. More than just possible, I believe it is the goal with the best kind of hidden treasure: no regrets.

BREAKING THROUGH THE SPIRAL CEILING

AN AMERICAN WOMAN BECOMES A DNA SCIENTIST

CHAPTER 1
CLOSED DOOR, OPENED DOOR IN WOODS HOLE

In Woods Hole, Massachusetts, I made a commitment to science that carried me though the rest of my career. Recently I read Linda Lear's biography of Rachel Carson, and was delighted to see Carson had been attracted to science by Woods Hole too. For the summer after my freshman year at Goucher College, I applied to study Marine Ecology at Marine Biological Laboratory (MBL) in Woods Hole. My Goucher "big sister" gave me the MBL brochure. The picture on the cover glowed with weather-beaten grey clapboard buildings against a dark blue sea. I had never seen water that color; it immediately appealed to me. The Goucher Biological Sciences department wanted to send junior and senior majors, not rising sophomores with no declared major. But I was the sole applicant that year, so they sent me.

In the bright sunshine, inhaling a sea breeze scented with algae and adventure, I looked up at a tall, rectangular building resembling a courthouse, Lillie Laboratory. Across the top I read, "Study Nature, Not Books," quoting Louis Agassiz, a former director of the MBL. My course met in the weathered wooden "Old Main," across the street. I studied nature all day, and much of the night, collecting and experimenting with animals and plants from different habitats on Cape Cod.

We learned to isolate marine algae in pure cultures from a scientist from Woods Hole Oceanographic Institution (WHOI). I sat in the rectangular lab on the second floor, looking out at the white stilt-legged *Fundulus* fishtanks in the courtyard below. He told us what to do, then he gave each pair a mixed culture. In the center of the long table topped with tan linoleum sat stacks of supplies. I sucked one cell into a narrow tube and released it into clean, sterile sea water. After a couple of minutes of watching the desired cell swim around vigorously, I sucked it out of the water and put it into fresh sterile sea water. By the time I had moved the cell six or seven times, all of the tiny bacteria and other algal cells were left behind. It was fun for me, but people who weren't good with their hands had trouble catching the cell they wanted.

Then he showed us his pure cultures. I particularly liked the dinoflagellates. We learned that these algae get a jolt of minerals from the ocean floor, grow rapidly, choke out other algae, and turn the sea red. They cause "killer red tides"; their poison kills fish. Under high power in our compound microscopes, we saw their complex inner structures. Each dinoflagellate was one intricate cell that looked like an Escher drawing executed in luxuriant olive, soft spruce, flashing diamond, iridescent chartreuse. They were bioluminescent too, resembling shooting stars in the dark surf.

Every Marine Ecology student had to perform a three week project. I gathered my courage, walked down the street to WHOI and asked the man who had taught us about algae, "Do you have any projects that you need help with?"

He raised his bushy eyebrows and ran his hand through his thick blond hair. After a minute that seemed eternal to me, he smiled and asked if I'd like to look at photosynthesis in isolated diatoms and dinoflagellates.

I said "Yes!" before he had even finished his sentence. Dinoflagellates were my favorite algae and I thought diatoms were cool, sheltered inside a clear glass box. Photosynthesis meant we would look at their biochemistry—great!

He said, "You'll have to use radioactive carbon dioxide and different light intensities, okay?"

"No problem," I said. But after a moment, I asked, "How can I get different light intensities?"

"Just use neutral density filters," he said. I knew nothing about neutral density filters, but I didn't want to reveal that ignorance. So I walked back to MBL and asked Don, the TA for Marine Ecology, "Do you have any neutral density filters?" He handed me a box of metal sheets perforated with tiny holes. Aha, so that's what they were. I could cover the bottles of algae with these filters. Some kept out almost all light while others let through a lot of light. I also used unfiltered bottles where the algae received full sunshine. Finally, I used dark bottles for controls. Algae in dark bottles can't do photosynthesis.

Each experiment day, I assembled my light and dark bottles. I added radioactive tracer that turned into radioactive sugar during photosynthesis. I placed the bottles in the sun on the WHOI dock and while they worked, I brooded over the algae, urging their tiny chloroplasts to capture light energy to make food and watching the oceanographic vessels prepare to go out to sea. Surprisingly, filtered sunlight was more effective than straight sunlight for photosynthesis by my algae.

I presented my findings along with the other Marine Ecology students. I wasn't sure why the filtered ones worked better. My supervisor was interested; he suggested that these algae might occur down beneath the surface layer of the ocean, so they got less light that they'd get at the surface. He said, "Laura, your data are surprising but they look very convincing." I was glad I hadn't become interested in sea snails; one student collected their droppings and examined them under the microscope. Another student gave glow beads to tube worms. They incorporated beads into their tubes if nothing else was available. I felt that my project was much more molecular and therefore much more interesting.

As summer waned, I daydreamed about the upcoming cruise. The Marine Ecology course was six weeks long. The lab brochure said that anyone in Marine Ecology who wished to stay an extra week could cruise on the *Atlantis*. On TV, I had seen this famous WHOI ketch fitted out for oceanographic research. It had four off-white sails, gleaming golden decks, and a white hull contrasting with dark blue water. I felt ready for the trip because my class had practiced with standard oceanography equipment: Nansen bottles for sampling water at particular depths, Secchi disks for testing water clarity. The cruise ship was far bigger than the ones we used, so we could sample from deep water, not just the shelves near the shore. It promised to be a first rate mixture of enjoyment and learning.

A course instructor, John D. Palmer, who asked us students to call him Jack, noticed that I knew the radiochemical assay for photosynthesis. Jack was a tall young man with a ready smile, dancing dark brown eyes, and shiny black hair that lay flat against his head.

He invited me to stay for another six weeks of research following the formal course, and see if photosynthesis followed tidal timing. I was thrilled at the opportunity, but I checked with Palmer to make sure it was alright for me to go on the cruise. It was. I could stay in Woods Hole for the rest of the summer. Life was beautiful.

About a week before the cruise, I walked down to WHOI to ask my project supervisor what I should be doing to get ready for the trip. He said, "Oh, I'm sorry, you can't go."

"Why?"

"The working sailors know that women on ships are bad luck, so they refuse to sail if women are on board."

I flinched, then turned and ran out of WHOI. *Bad luck? How unscientific.* He had let down the honor of science, which claims that everything you believe must be proved. How could these scientists let the sailors get away with it? I ran back to my dorm, sat on my bed with my fists clenched and cried, grieving for my impossible future in biological oceanography. Then came anger, because I couldn't see why he accepted the word of sailors about "luck," unless he too thought it better to leave the women at home. Hadn't I produced wonderful data from my project, data that he had found interesting? Why wasn't I worthy to go?

No one else was in the dorm at that hour; the girls whose summer job was to clean up the dorms had finished and everyone else was in lab. A big fly persistently battered itself against the screen in the window. I finally pulled myself together. I told myself I had a great opportunity here to study something exciting with Palmer. I wouldn't have to face the man from WHOI every day.

My feelings toward Marine Ecology never recovered. During the rest of the summer in Woods Hole, each time I saw a blonde man about the height of my WHOI supervisor, I cringed inside. He never asked if I was okay or if I had recovered from my upset feelings. I never talked with him again except for distant greetings.

I told my research mentor, Jack Palmer, my arguments for changing the rule about women on the cruise. He heard me out, but didn't say anything about his own feelings. I tried to avoid the WHOI dock and kept my eyes down as I passed the *Atlantis*. I froze the bad feelings away in the bottom of my mind, a TV dinner waiting to be reflected upon later by my adult mind.

When I turned away from marine ecology I fell in love with DNA, in the Woods Hole Friday night lectures, and later by auditing the Physiology course. DNA: how to describe the pull it exerted on the rest of my life? DNA encodes all we can do, be, and become. It encompasses the past, back through time to the primordial ooze. We share the genes of those first organisms. Our genes encode our possible futures, many actions waiting to be switched on. DNA is a beautiful molecule. Starting with Francis

Crick's wife Odile, an artist who drew DNA for Watson and Crick's paper, many artists have incorporated the double helix into their work, unable to resist its shape.

For me as a biologist, its beauty lies in that beautiful shape to be sure, but it also lies in its meaning. Because the two strands fit together like two matching puzzle pieces, when the two pull apart, each shape can only fit a similar partner to the one it lost. So two copies of the double helix are easy to make, perfectly with no mistakes. You can transmit your DNA, it will work as well for your children as it has for you.

But why do you have a drive to pass it on? Each segment of DNA contains the directions for constructing a protein, written in the genetic code. Proteins do all the work of the cell. Having the right protein at the right time is essential to life, and the gene, with its disposable copy called messenger RNA, makes that possible. The word "potential" best expresses DNA to me. The regulation of how that potential is realized has fascinated me for my entire career, and still fascinates my college students today.

Since I could not sail the seas, I could choose genes instead. I was about to make that choice, but I had another flirtation with ecology first.

Chapter 2
Finding Problems at Goucher College

Becoming a scientist isn't a slam dunk. I was a late-blooming scientist, even with encouragement from my chemical engineer father. I had a hard time seeing where scientists found the questions or problems they studied. People think science is all about the answers, but if you want to practice science, finding the problems is more important. That issue came to a boil in 1962, during my sophomore year at Goucher College in Baltimore, before my second summer in Woods Hole. Helene Guttman came to substitute for a professor who was on leave. She was five feet of dynamite, never still and always talking. She had short, curly light brown hair that had split ends and flew everywhere. Helene knew it all. I don't mean she was a know-it-all, but just try to mention something you think she hadn't heard of. Of course she was from New York, and that helps when you want to know it all. Maybe it's the confidence they get from the perception that New York is the hub of the universe. "I work on pteridine pigments," she said, and I'm sure she gloried in the fact that not one person in ten who heard the name of the pigments could spell the word.

I diffidently mentioned to her that I needed more work hours, and she said, "I have several bottles of frozen flies you can behead for me, if you want."

Oh, boy, not really what I had in mind. But it was money. So I worked for her cutting off the heads of frozen fruit flies. She wanted the heads because most of the flies' colored pigments were in the huge eyes. I must admit, at times when I was frustrated, I dubbed these flies with the names of certain professors, just before relieving them of their heads. As I beheaded flies, Helene talked about science; she often said, "Now *that* would make a good project!" She mentioned many interesting questions in biology, or areas that we didn't yet understand. She spouted these unsolved problems from every pore.

At some point, I asked her my naïve question. "Where do problems come from? How do you think up good problems to base a project on?" She looked at me with amazement and didn't answer. I guess she didn't know, since it came so naturally to her. She said, "Here, I will put up a list on my bookshelf of problems that would be interesting to work on." Of course, those were *her* problems.

With today's eyes, I think that I sensed that I had been filling in the details in grand designs of science thought out by others, according to Thomas Kuhn's ideas in *The Structure of Scientific Revolutions*. Kuhn suggested that some fields of science had not yet put together a grand design. In other fields, people had agreed about the overview and were just doing normal research, checking off points and filling in details. Kuhn explained that it was possible to work in a disorganized field, figure out the next great generalization, and have a huge impact on science. I imagined a TV game show where the prize was a major scientific discovery hidden behind a golden door. I wanted a way to find the end of the thread that would lead to that golden door behind which an important mystery of nature was hiding.

I heard an amusing apocryphal anecdote about problem selection by Nobel laureates, Melvin Calvin and Arthur Kornberg.

They sat in a bar discussing what to work on early in their careers. They supposedly decided that Calvin would discover how carbon was captured in photosynthesis, and Arthur Kornberg would discover how DNA was copied for inheritance. They did, and voila! Nobel prizes for both. I heard that they later wore satin prize-fighter robes with the years of their Nobel prizes on them to a Stanford University event, flaunting scientific machismo. Is this true? Who knows, but it's the kind of legendary talk about science that young scientists hear. It's a story full of the male show-off, competitive mentality, but as a woman I didn't resonate to that aspect. For me, the moral seemed to be that if you found the right problem, you would be spectacularly successful in science.

I thought picking a momentous problem was important, but I just didn't know how to do it. I wondered about my naïve question, decapitated some flies, decapitated some more flies, and looked at Helene's posted "problems list" to see if it would suggest where her ideas originated. It didn't. I sighed and went back to the fly guillotine.

Finally, almost imperceptibly, I crossed that line. I came to know enough about biology that I started asking questions. The phrase 'critical mass' is out of favor since atomic energy isn't politically correct, but it seemed like I needed to collect a critical mass of information, and then it would start a chain reaction in my brain. By watching this reaction ferment, I would see where the connections were missing or unclear or where they implied a piece of the puzzle that was missing. Using some more male imagery, you could call the insight a bombshell. From fly heads to bombshells was my path, then, and because Helene had no real answers for me, I had to find my own way.

I first noticed that the barrier was broken when I jotted down ideas for research while reading an Embryology text alone in my room. I was so pleased when it hit me what I had done that I danced a jig, clicking my heels until the students downstairs banged on the ceiling.

The process I went through, trying to understand where questions and problems come from, has made me more interested in students trying to make this leap. Students want to start with a pre-existing problem; it's a struggle to get them to take a risk. They typically look for their own golden doors when they start to design a senior thesis question they want to answer. It's particularly hard for very bright students, who easily criticize published experiments; quick critical analysis can nip creativity in the bud. Working with these students, I can suggest that they keep their critical facility leashed until they have produced a lot of creative thoughts, and use it only to choose among them. If they criticize each idea as they produce it, their imaginations appear stunted and they sometimes give up and propose to develop the thoughts arising directly from a prior student's project. I have come to recognize this issue and try to forestall premature criticism before it happens with current students.

I can say I'm a scientist, and proudly so, but I'm also a teacher who wants to produce more scientists. I exulted when the PhD advisor of one of my former students said, "She was trembling with excitement when she told me about her results!" He begged me to send him more students who understand the thrill of research, and I know why. One of the joys of my academic life is working with students who are in the process of playing my imaginary TV game show and finding their own threads leading them to the golden doors they want to open.

CHAPTER 3
FIRST RESEARCH PUBLICATION—WOODS HOLE REDUX

Jack Palmer invited me back to MBL the next summer to be a TA for Marine Ecology and research algal photosynthetic rhythms. The second year, I had time to audit the lectures in the Physiology course. Interactions of molecules were just as exciting as the insides of algal cells. I imagined proteins and nucleic acids docking to each other and upon receiving a signal, releasing to float away like spaceships in a dream sky.

Later on, the material of Physiology would be called molecular biology. That name was not yet invented. It had to survive calumny as many geneticists and biochemists insisted they were NOT molecular biologists. Then it rose triumphant as the name of the interdisciplinary field of genetic biochemistry.

Physiology taught us about separating molecules on columns and gradients, purifying them, and putting their capabilities to the test. It seemed that getting a biochemical function to occur in the test tube, starting from known, purified components, was the main goal of the field. I understood the material without really trying. Once I started studying the concepts, they all flowed out like a river from a spring, so connected that I needed no effort to understand. But others struggled. A Brown graduate student, listening to a lecture by a famous protein chemist, asked, "How can you plot enzyme activity versus tube number? That's meaningless."

I didn't hesitate to tell him, "As the sample is washed through a column, fractions are collected in order in numbered tubes. That's what he means by tube number." But how did I know? I had not tried this method myself, it just made sense to me.

Much of the physiology course was an ardent presentation of reductionism, the approach that insists that if we completely understand the individual molecules, the way that the whole cell works will be self-evident. I loved the linear thinking, the inferences. This logic was different from the memorizing and sorting I had previously learned in biology. Here we could reason from first principles; here it all fit together.

But there were holistic threads in the Physiology class as well. Albert Szent-Gyorgyi, who discovered and purified Vitamin C, lived in Woods Hole. In the dining hall, gossip relayed news about him to the Woods Hole newcomers. He swam several miles in the cold Atlantic every day. He leapt up onto lecture desks with a single bound. He bought his mansion on Penzance Point in Wood Hole with the proceeds of his Nobel Prize.

Szent-Gyorgyi lectured in Physiology twice. Once he told us a long anecdote about how he purified vitamin C. He was sure it would fluoresce, so everything he purified for a long time was fluorescent. But these compounds were all contaminants of his rubber tubing. "The vitamin itself was not fluorescent at all!" He stopped, ruffled up his halo of white hair, and looked at us with a twinkle in his eye. "What do you think of that?" he asked, and burst out with a raucous cackle. He never gave us a moral. But his story reminded me of a saying of my father's when he was pretending to be a back-country farmer, "It ain't what you don't know that'll get you in trouble. It's what you know that ain't so."

Another day, Szent-Gyorgyi appeared with his white halo of hair neatly combed, in his bright yellow shirt and khaki walking shorts, bounding about the front of the room like a man 40 years younger. He told us about the proteins actin and myosin cooperating in muscle contraction, powered by ATP. His biochemist colleague put actin and myosin in a small quartz box or cuvette, placed it in a machine that measures light, and then shot in ATP. The machine recorded that there was no change in light absorbance.

He told us the biochemist said, "You're wrong, Albert, NOTHING happens when you add ATP to actin and myosin." He said, "I brought him a beaker of the same muscle proteins and a pipette of ATP and asked him to squirt the ATP in. And he did. And the solution contracted into a ball." The whole place broke up laughing. Again, no moral was forthcoming. What was he trying to tell us? That our own senses were better guides to molecules than machine readings? Or to use all the ways you can to observe molecules, since different ways give different information?

During Physiology, I was sucked deeper and deeper into the mysteries of molecules passing information from one to another. I was fascinated by genes and their effects. I was learning the secrets of life, seeing behind the veil of nature. How seductive; how irresistible.

The second summer, my new friend Susie and I talked a lot; we liked to sing folk songs and we swapped the new ones we heard. But I got involved with John, a good-looking graduate student. Soon Susie was disgusted. I skipped times we were supposed to get together so I could do things with John. He was demanding and didn't like me to do things with anyone but him. For a while, I didn't mind.

One night in late July, John tried to rape me in his laboratory. He told me that he had a squid in his seawater tank, and a dish marbled with areas of sand colored or mud colored background. He said we could put the squid in the dish and watch its colored cells contract and expand under the microscope. But when we got to the laboratory, he tried to grab me. I backed away, telling him

'No!" He chased me all around the lab, tearing my T shirt whenever he got close. I was gasping for air when he finally cornered me and threw me on the floor. As he dropped down beside me, I slithered away. I escaped through a door into the Invertebrate Biology teaching lab where I stole a towel to replace my shirt.

I wish I could tell you about my deep reaction to this rape attempt. I wasn't introspective, and I thought he was just acting out attitudes towards women that seemed "normal." The subliminal messages said that if I couldn't put up with caveman behavior, I wasn't tough enough to make it in science. I packed this rape attempt in that freezer at the bottom of my mind along with the denial of the *Atlantis* cruise. It never came back to haunt me until my daughter was 18 and I considered what might happen to her when I wasn't around. Then I began to get angry at John and at MBL. But John and MBL had been out of my life a long time. I realized I hadn't been permanently harmed and put the memory to rest. I figured out that I could help Heather: we enrolled in a women's self defense class together.

After dinner at the MBL dining hall each evening, there was lots of science talk among the students. On the porch one night in summer, 1962, I heard comments like this: "Yes, Molecular Biology is dead! All the important stuff has already been discovered, didn't you hear what Sydney Brenner said? Go into neurobiology, where there are still basic ideas to uncover, before it's too late! Brenner's going to map the fate of every cell developing in *C. elegans* and find out where all the neurons come from!"

The round worm (*C. elegans*) is a famous model organism today, but at the time I hated to think we were all going to stop working on microorganisms just because Brenner said so. He probably had never even seen a dinoflagellate. No one said, "So what if Brenner is a friend of Crick's? He could be wrong!" I didn't say it either, but my mind was shouting it silently. I wasn't going to give up on DNA and follow this new fashion.

I couldn't believe that the field I had yet to enter was already dead. It wasn't. Important discoveries were coming, like split genes, catalytic and inhibitory RNA, and down-regulation of genes by scrunching up the DNA in chromatin. And molecular biology techniques revolutionized every field of biology and medicine. Informational molecules provided a handle to understand it all. But I might have been able make more important discoveries if I had listened to advice about *C. elegans*. Who knows?

My second summer in Woods Hole was a success scientifically. Jack Palmer, Father Dennis Zusy, and I collaborated on our project. We took samples every six hours, day and night. In between, we cleaned up our equipment, collected data, and prepared for the next sampling period. Once, Jack had to send to the dorm to get me out for a sample when I overslept. I think it was only once.

We examined rhythms in photosynthetic capacity in single celled algae during several light/dark cycles. We found out how "smart" the algae really were. Their capacity to use light rose every day before the sunrise, anticipating their need for it. We did show that the biochemistry is hooked to the clock, but not that it ran the clock. Others discovered the clock biochemistry many years later. But our own experiment resulted in a paper in *Nature*: my first paper ever, in a "high impact journal." I was inordinately proud of that paper, even before I knew what a special journal it was. It seemed to prove I was a scientist.

About to start my junior year in college, I told people I was going into "biochemistry." I had declared a Biological Sciences major and planned to take plenty of chemistry too. But after that summer of auditing Physiology and working on my first paper, I committed to study the beautiful molecule DNA, its inheritance and expression.

CHAPTER 4
WHAT GRADUATE MENTOR?

At Goucher College, my thesis advisor, Miss Ann Lacy told me how important it was to pick the right graduate mentor. Ann, stocky with bristling short red hair and a forthright manner, had experienced repressive tactics mixed with interesting research when she studied for her PhD with David Bonner at Yale.

She told us about male scientists who asked about her plans for marriage and children before admitting her to graduate school, and about tough questions asked of her in seminars, possibly to embarrass her. Once, I asked Lacy why she told us so much about bad treatment of women in graduate school. She looked a bit thoughtful, and then said, "I think you need to know what it is really like because you should decide in advance whether or not you're tough enough to take it."

Obviously, the days of fighting "it" or making "it" illegal had not yet dawned. The popular catalyst of feminism in the US, Betty Friedan's *Feminine Mystique*, came out in 1963, my senior year at Goucher, but I was completely unaware of the nascent feminist movement at first. My graduate school search was the year before her book was published. Discriminating against women wasn't yet illegal, and I ran into it along the way. I hated finding men who thought women could not make it in science, and usually wanted to "shake the dust of the place off my feet" when I encountered that kind of treatment, just as I had with Marine Ecology earlier.

In the summer after junior year, I decided I could take it. I had spent that summer in New York, doing research with Ruth Sager at Columbia University and reading articles in the Columbia Library to prepare for my senior thesis project. I felt ready to commit to future research and (I hoped) teaching. I wanted to see the faculty at graduate schools who were my potential mentors, and who would also be considering me as a graduate student. I wanted to feel comfortable with the mentor, to be able to talk science with him. Unfortunately, back in 1963 there were no "hers" to consider for a mentor in my field. Women worked as research associates with major professors, not as independent faculty members who could take graduate students.

My first hypothesis about my ideal mentor: I'd choose someone doing something really new and interesting. I had studied molecular genetics of fungi at Goucher College, getting ready for a senior thesis project, and I was drawn to find out how organisms regulated their chemical reactions. For my senior thesis, I hypothesized that a newly discovered biochemical pathway could run forwards and backwards, in response to demand. The pathway had three end products: tryptophan, tyrosine, and phenylalanine. I increased the concentration of one end product and limited the other two, hoping that the overflowing excess of one could be converted to the others. Now we know that pathways that produce such end products are not reversible, but the pathways had just been discovered then, and no one knew how their flow was regulated. I planned to do a factorial combination of concentrations of the three end products and use statistics to test the results.

Besides biochemical genetics, I also found some newly proposed ideas about protein level regulation interesting. So I thought about working with Arthur Pardee. I had been to Johns Hopkins to hear him talk about how the activity of enzymes could be turned on and off by feedback inhibition mechanisms, without affecting their structure. He described how this feedback inhibition could coordinate entire biochemical pathways that had to work together. I have always been taken with integrating ideas, about how the parts of the cell cooperate. His work seemed well done, well designed and convincing. I also liked how he presented himself. He was not, as we would have said, "a pompous ass" but was open to suggestions and interested in discussing ideas, not ramming his points down the throats of the audience. So, I wrote to Princeton requesting a graduate catalog.

"Dear Miss Livingston," they replied, "We have not sent the catalog and graduate application which you requested. Unless there is a peculiar need for our facilities, we do not consider admission of women to the graduate program here." Here was another item for the freezer at the bottom of my mind.

That letter took away all my interest in the place, just as biting into an unripe persimmon once turned me off the fruit for life. No welcome mat there, it seemed. While I might have been able to convince them that I did have a "peculiar need" for Princeton, my desire to go there was gone. Today, Shirley Tilghman, a prominent molecular biologist, is the President of Princeton. I'm sure women applicants are encouraged today.

My second hypothesis (ironically): using the "old boy network." Miss Lacy knew people in fungal biochemical genetics because she had done her PhD with David Bonner, so her acquaintances would be a good cohort to search for an accessible advisor. I thought of David Bonner and Charles Yanofsky in California. They were "Bonner kingdom" members whom I had seen at the American Society for Microbiology meetings. They talked fascinating science, about how the molecules of life worked, and I liked them.

Trailways Bus Company had a "see the country for $100" fare. I could go to California and meet both Bonner and Yanofsky and look at their schools. Once I decided to go West, I also thought of Caltech, home of the golden helix outside the biology buildings. My attraction to Caltech was more related to my first hypothesis, that I wanted to study something new and exciting. There, former physicist, Max Delbruck had enticed many people into science, with his elegant experiments using phage, the viruses that infect bacteria.

Because all the rest were in California, I thought I would add Berkeley, with no real hypothesis about how that related to graduate mentors. Then, it was a hotbed of war resistance, which I was "into" much more than my Dad was happy about. Mario Savio was famous for his rants at the Berkeley campus, and I thought it might be fun to hear him. Of course, there was good biology there too, but I have to confess it took a back seat to the anti-war aspects.

I paid my $100 and hopped on board in Charlotte, N.C., in August, 1963. I rode to California, never stopping to spend the night at all. I just leaned the bus seat back and covered myself up with my rain coat and slept as best I could. The sun had risen but the weather was overcast with a "marine layer" when I arrived in San Diego. I took a city bus out to the newly formed biology department of UCSD, then located at Scripps Institution of Oceanography. The SIO is right on the most beautiful beach in La Jolla, called La Jolla Shores. I could hardly take my eyes off the turquoise water shading to dark blue, seen through every window.

Potential mentor David Bonner, and I talked a long time. What struck me about him was that he actually talked science with me. It wasn't just show and tell. "Here is what we just found that is really interesting," he said, "The enzyme proteins are separate in bacteria but the genes and their proteins have fused together in our fungus. But in *Sordaria*, another fungus, a group in England found them separated. That would be a big problem for our theory that there's an evolutionary trend towards fusion, don't you think? What kind of experiment should we do now, repeat what we heard or look at a different organism?"

A lot of male biologists never ask females what they think, although most love to tell us females what they think. Bonner treated me like most mentors treated a male graduate student, and I loved it! I also enjoyed talking with another faculty member studying fungal metabolism. I stayed with Judy, a graduate student at UCSD, who took me surfing on La Jolla Shores beach with some friends. So I enjoyed the visit there very much, and felt sure that Bonner would be high on my graduate advisor wish list.

Next, I migrated north to Caltech on a rerun of my first hypothesis about looking for something new. Delbruck and others there were connected to the Watson-Crick grapevine and were frequently in the midst of important new experiments on genetic information. On arriving in Los Angeles, I found it dead set against efficient public transportation. Getting out to Caltech proved to be a three hour assignment. But I finally spied the golden double helix that graced the entrance to the Caltech biology buildings.

My host professor un-welcomed me by saying, "…now before you tell me anything about yourself, I want to let you know that we just don't admit women here. Don't take it personally, you're planning very interesting senior thesis work and I'm looking forward to talking with you about it." I was stunned. He had agreed to meet me, and after Bonner's interview I didn't see this reaction coming.

I said, "Never mind," and rose to leave, but he urged me to stay and we did talk science for about an hour. My planned senior thesis on how biochemical pathways might reverse to respond to food needs of the organism interested him; he was impressed that I had put together the whole aromatic amino acid biosynthesis pathway from many separate research articles. The talk ended and I walked sadly out thinking there was no way was I going to Caltech. I marveled that the professor had seemed so interested in my work but wasn't willing to help me get admitted to his graduate program. I packed one more souvenir away in the freezer in my mind, and that was the end of the hypothesis that I should work on something hot and new. I was left with the second hypothesis that I should work with a mentor found through Lacy's connections.

I boarded another bus and took off northward for the Bay Area, not yet the biotechnology capital of the world. Following up on Lacy connections, I stopped off at Stanford, along the western shore of San Francisco Bay to visit the laboratory of Charles Yanofsky who was working on the genes encoding the enzymes for making tryptophan in bacteria. Yanofsky had a magnetic personality and when we talked, he made me see the excitement of what his laboratory was doing. I've always enjoyed scientists who can sell their projects, almost in a "used car salesman" sort of way, and Yanofsky had that ability. I can't recall his exact words, but it was something like this.

"How can a mutation suppress the effect of a mutation in a different gene? It's voodoo. Can't happen. Sounds like 'action at a distance' that the physicists are always jabbering about. But, it does happen and we're about to find the exact mechanism."

Finding the exact mechanism sounded so linear, so much like Watson and Crick, that I wanted to be a part of the action. He didn't ask me about my own thesis or talk science with me in the sense of exchanging ideas, but I loved the beauty of Stanford's campus and he was a "Bonner kingdom" person, after all. So even though Yanofsky's laboratory was in a dark corridor and not too up-to-date looking, Yanofsky still jumped to the top of my list as potential mentor. The excitement of his molecular genetic thinking was more important to me than personal encouragement to me to talk science. The hypothesis that connections would yield a good mentor was supported again.

I stayed in the Bay area to visit Berkeley and heard Mario Savio speak against the Vietnam War, but wasn't taken with Berkeley's possibilities for graduate work. There were at least five biology departments, and it seemed too fragmented.

Soon after I got back, I applied for a graduate fellowship from NSF. Because Yanofsky at Stanford was my first choice, I put him down on the forms. But before I did, I checked with NSF to make sure that I could change my mind later. Boy, would that prove significant.

I had left off one important person: David Bonner's former Yale competitor, who was also a Lacy connection from her PhD at Yale. My final test of the hypothesis that a perfect mentor came through networking was to visit Norman Giles at Yale. I went up to New Haven by train near the end of the first semester of senior year. I liked Yale; all of the undergraduate colleges were spread out over New Haven, which I had heard was unattractive, but I didn't find it so. I really enjoyed the big square park in the center of the town.

I stayed with Mary Case, a friend of Ann Lacy's from graduate school. Mary was a senior postdoctoral associate with Norman Giles. Her position was the typical woman's position in Biology at Yale in the 1960's. When Norman moved to University of Georgia in the 1970's, one of the things he asked for was a faculty position for Mary. In Biology at Yale at that time, there was only one female faculty member, and you wouldn't know she was a woman to see her. She had delicate birdlike features, but had a man's haircut and wore men's clothes and shoes. "Men's SHOES," became a catch phrase of some of the women graduate students. Other women there, including one who had received highest honors at Yale for her PhD work, were senior post doctoral associates with male faculty members.

Beatrice Sweeney, who had created devices to measure oxygen production by individual cells, and used them to show that biological rhythms happen even in single cells, was just a senior postdoctoral fellow. By taking postdoctoral research positions, these women got to know everything going on in their fields world-wide, were invited to speak at meetings, received funds through their professors' grants, published papers, and never had to teach or be on committees. Sounds great, but they were never the ones recognized by National Academy of Science, Nobel Prizes, etc. It was the professor who would reap the major recognition for their work.

At Yale, I met with Norman Giles, who had a Southern charm that I enjoyed. He started off on the wrong tack by saying he was pleased with my high Graduate Record Exam scores, and that he had been advocating for a bigger role for GRE scores in admissions. I was profoundly suspicious of standardized test scores, maybe as much because I always did well on them as because the discriminatory aspects of the questions were beginning to be noticed. Giles did talk science with me, and I told him some interesting findings from my senior thesis experiments. I had found that the pathway would not reverse. Instead, the best growth was when all three end products were at the same concentration. We discussed my results and tried to explain them. We decided that the balance requirement was probably due to competition between the three products for transport system that brought them into the cells.

"That's interesting for us because we're growing the same mutants," he drawled. "But I don't know if you can get it published. I'm afraid it would be like trying to publish the boiling point of water." That phrase was prophetic; we did not get the results published.

He told me about the new work in his laboratory on how groups of enzymes that stuck together might channel compounds into one of their many possible fates. I found that fascinating, and so did many others. Later on, those experiments were the basis of Norman's election to the National Academy of Science. After that final visit, Yale moved up my list to become tied for second with UCSD, right after Stanford.

The exploration validated the networking approach to finding a mentor. All of my best prospective mentors were Lacy connections. Neither of my potential graduate schools with mentors that Lacy didn't know panned out. But, even among the choices for mentors with connections, I didn't go where I had planned. In *Composing a Life*, Mary Bateson described her creative interaction with random events that pushed her down unexpected paths. She used the new raw material, with her basic approach, to "compose" the outcome. My final graduate school selection had that random quality.

I ended up going to Yale after all. Right before Christmas, I got a letter accepting me to Stanford graduate program. Noticing that it said nothing about Yanofsky, I wrote and asked if I would be able to work in his lab. The answer was no, he had accepted a Stanford undergraduate who already worked with him.

Next, I chose UCSD, selecting the opportunity to work with Bonner along with the surf and sand of La Jolla. When I received an NSF Graduate Fellowship, I designated it to UCSD and happily planned to join the Bonner laboratory. Ann Lacy commented, "Too bad Bonner moved from Yale, or you could have a blue PhD robe like mine, which you always admired."

My selected mentor, David Bonner, went camping in the desert and caught an infection. When added to his ongoing Hodgkin's lymphoma, which had been under control for many years, that infection caused his death. I was profoundly sorry for his family. His death presented me with a dilemma. I had really only wanted to work with him, out of the few faculty at UCSD in those early days. But I had already written to the other places I had applied and said I wasn't coming.

At the national microbiology meeting in Washington, DC that spring, Norman Giles came over to talk with Ann Lacy and me and told me that he could get my admission to Yale reactivated if I was interested. I checked with NSF again, and was told that considering the circumstances, they would let me make yet another change in my fellowship location. So I went to Yale, home of the blue academic robe, after all.

What I composed, given Yale's resources, was a graduate training broadly based in biology and including ethnomusicology, harking back to Goucher's vision of the turf of the liberal arts. I threw myself into a novel research area with lots of promise. I took Dean John Perry Miller's seminar on college governance. I worked with friends to organize anti-war teach-ins. I chaired the Biology Graduate Student Association. Looking back now, I see myself preparing to be a biologist with a wide view of the field, a person of diverse interests beyond science, a person who wanted to know how academia worked. My life composition, later revealed to produce a liberal arts college professor and an academic Vice President, drew support from practically everything I did at Yale.

CHAPTER 5
SEXUAL HARASSMENT

I arrived at Yale with almost no money. By getting profoundly tired of eggs, I survived the first month and received my first stipend check. My classes were interesting, I performed a few experiments, and I began to make friends with people. I didn't think it would be a problem to be nice to a priest. I had been friends with two kind, gentle, humorous priests at Woods Hole, one of whom was a coauthor on the *Nature* paper we had published. At Yale, there was a priest among the students associated with my advisor, Norman Giles. He joked around with everyone and wore regular clothes except for a clerical collar. He used a good many German words, calling the heavy gloves we used to unload hot equipment from the steam sterilizer "handshue" and so forth. He asked me to go out to lunch on a Saturday when we were both working in the laboratory and I agreed.

After the lunch, which was very pleasant, he said, "You know I'm interested in you. Why don't you ever give me any encouragement?"

"B—but you're a priest," I stammered. "But I'm still a man, aren't I?"

Well, not to me, I thought, but didn't say it. I just said, "I'm sorry, but it's impossible."

He said nothing, but took me back to the laboratory, let me

off, and drove away. I thought no more about it then. But, many times I had to work late at the lab. I began to sense someone following me home through the darkness. I rented an extremely cheap apartment above George and Harry's bar, in a building that was condemned but not yet torn down. It was two rooms: a kitchen and a room with a couch and a bed in it, with a shared bathroom across the hall. If I ever got bored studying at night, I went down to the bar to have a beer or make them laugh by ordering tea. Sometimes the Yale Russian Chorus practiced there, or it might be full of young ice hockey players from Bridgeport or race car drivers. It was another world, often seeming more real than the science world I was in most of the time.

My apartment was about a mile from where our laboratory was located, and many of the streets had few or no streetlights. Once I had begun to worry about a follower, I tried to see if anyone was behind me, but it was hard to tell. I got the impression sometimes that I could spot someone lurking, but I couldn't tell who it was for a long time. Then, one night I spotted the priest clearly, as he was passing under a dim streetlight.

I was afraid he meant me some harm, but there was no way I could stop doing my research at night, since the postdoctoral fellows used all the equipment in the day. The priest was a stocky man, tall and broad, in good physical shape. Avoiding him, I took different routes. But I spotted him again one night, not a half block behind me. Running away from John had worked in Woods Hole, but there was no good way to escape here, his stalking seemed relentless.

Finally I told my office mate, Karim Ali El Eryani, a very level headed young man from Yemen. "Karim, I'm afraid of the priest. He follows me home at night."

Karim said, "Well, let me get a couple of people together so someone can always walk home with you." In the end, it was almost always Karim himself who kindly did it.

"There he is," he said one night about a week later. We had just rounded the corner at Jonathan Edwards College and started down my street. Karim looked back along our route and spotted the priest in pursuit.

"Oh, no, I thought if someone was with me he would stop," I said.

"Well, maybe he can't, he must have lost his head after all or he wouldn't be doing this," Karim responded.

I was glad Karim had seen him. In those days, men often said women were making up their night-worries. It was bad news that the priest had not stopped. Still we didn't tell Norman Giles, and I never confronted the priest himself.

Another male graduate student who sometimes walked home with me said, "It's not unheard of; a graduate student who was here a couple of years ago was following Lorraine around and stealing her notes."

"Did anyone do anything to help?"

"No, she didn't ask, and we didn't know what kind of relationship they had or might have had, so we stayed out of it," he told me.

The situation with the priest ended naturally, to my relief, but now I wonder how it all turned out for him. I went to Europe that summer for a month's vacation, and when I returned the priest was no longer there. I don't know if he left, was recalled, or was asked to leave, but I was very thankful that he was no longer around.

There was no sharing among the women graduate students about this kind of behavior and what to do about it. I believe that the idea of women's solidarity was not yet part of our understanding of the universe. We resisted the Eisenhower-era's program for our kitchen-wife fates, but we hadn't had our consciousness raised either. We were before the wave of Baby Boomers' with their understanding that they were to change the rules. We had to make it all up as we went along.

One time, I knew about a harassment of another woman in advance, and didn't do anything to stop it. I'm not at all proud of this, but from my subsequent reading, I can see that it's a well-known behavior pattern whereby early entrants into a previously closed society tend to cooperate with the oppressors. A faculty member who was very interested in young women (according to the grapevine) was appointed the Director of Graduate Study. He recruited a lot of attractive women to graduate study at Yale. One of the new female students was a blonde and some of the older male students thought she should lose some weight (why? I didn't ask then, more's the pity!) She wasn't really fat, just a little rounded. So, they started putting notes on her notebooks left in the library and her lab work station suggesting various diets and exercise programs and I think, providing insulting reasons why she should take them up. I didn't do anything to stop my friends from picking on her. It only made me feel slightly uneasy.

Back then, I took men's physical appraisal of women's worth for granted, and thought they had a right to leave these notes as long as it didn't threaten the woman physically. Of course, that was completely wrong; I'm sure it made her feel terrible, and might even have made her seriously consider a different career. I would hate to hear about something like this happening to one of my former students in graduate school, it makes me angry even to think about it. So why the anesthetized conscience then? I don't have the answer. Today, I don't see any papers by her on PubMed database. I hope it's because her name changed, and I wish I had spoken up and convinced them to leave her alone.

I encountered a "too fat" appraisal myself not long afterwards. In the stress of research and writing during my last year of graduate school, I gained weight. In spring of my fourth year of graduate school I went to the American Society for Microbiology Meeting and interviewed with a prospective postdoctoral advisor, Frank E. Young from Scripps Clinic and Research Foundation, in

La Jolla, CA, with whom I really wanted to work. After our meeting, he wrote me a short note saying that he would be glad to support my application for an NIH postdoctoral fellowship, but he wanted to tell me "purely from a medical perspective" that I needed to lose fifteen pounds. I just shrugged it off.

It happened that my NSF Graduate Fellowship funds ended two months before I had completed my work on the genetic basis of osmotic mutants and passed the thesis defense examination at Yale, and research associate Mary Case kindly offered me a place to stay and fed me during that time. Mary kept no snacks at home and ironically I lost the entire amount before I showed up for postdoctoral research.

Frank told me, when others weren't around, "You look a lot healthier now than you did when I interviewed you." This was not a come-on. He was a happily married man, but he felt it necessary to tell me anyway. Here is a true irony: Frank was one of the most color-blind and gender-blind persons I ever knew in science. He had a black postdoctoral fellow, Willie Brown, and a Latino technician, Luciano Arias, and they received high respect in his laboratory. Willie later went on to a faculty position at UCSD, I'm sure with Frank's support. And after all, Frank did take me as a post-doctoral fellow. I just wish he hadn't felt that my weight was within his supervisory capacity.

Another irony for me was receiving an indignant letter from Yale Biology Department about two years after I received my PhD, enclosing a questionnaire about treatment of women at Yale. The letter said that a complaint had been received, and the department had decided to survey its alumnae on their feelings, being sure that there was nothing to complain about. Yale had a lot to be proud of in their admission and funding of equal numbers of women and men at that time, unlike Princeton. And they didn't discriminate in advisor choices, teaching assignments, or class schedules. I never felt the cold wind of exclusion at Yale as I did when attending big scientific meetings later on in my career.

But sexual harassment was a problem. I thought about how there was nothing to encourage me to talk with my advisor when the priest stalked me. Was that just because there were no laws yet to protect women? That was certainly part of it. But the atmosphere didn't mitigate against sexual harassment; instead it was greeted with a wink and a nod.

I pointed out that the issue of female role models was a sore point too. And finally, I had to criticize how they helped women find jobs, as opposed to how they helped men. My male friends back then walked out of graduate school into great faculty positions at research universities like Stanford. Women were recommended to take postdoctoral fellowships. Today, it's the general rule that PhD graduates take one or more postdoctoral fellowships, but then it was only the rule for women. Where did these postdocs lead? In my graduate school class, mostly not to university appointments. Among men and women I knew well in my class and the two previous classes, seventy percent of the men and ten or twenty percent of the women (depending if you count research associate positions) got positions in research universities.

In later classes, as the wheel turned and the Kennedy/Johnson egalitarianism became more prevalent, others got more faculty positions. Especially the Yale women students who worked in Joseph Gall's laboratory group were successful in becoming outstanding faculty members at research universities, and he was recognized by the national cell biology society for his skill in mentoring women scientists. My advisor was not at all unkind or rude; he and I simply never developed a close scientific relationship.

I was lucky that I could talk science with both men and women who were research associates and graduate students in my department. We hashed over the beauty of DNA and the details of its regulation as well as physiology, ecology—the whole of biology was our turf. Our many gatherings to talk biology are a glowing memory, not dimmed by sexism. It was at Yale where I most fully realized my connections to the scientific community.

Harassment was surely a problem to me in my early time as a graduate student, but overt harassment wasn't a major theme in my life. My early lack of sensitivity to others' ideas and feelings probably insulated me from some intended harassment. In fact, I wasn't very sensitive to my own feelings either back then. Feelings only became important to me later in my life. Then, I was looking at my future through tunnel vision, and a few minor insults and snide remarks weren't all that noticeable to me. At Yale, in my second year, I went about my business learning about biology with a strong focus on the areas where I had to pass qualifying examinations. Nothing was going to get in the way of my success.

CHAPTER 6
QUALIFYING EXAMINATIONS

The qualifying examination was the chill maker, the hazing, the rite-of-passage when I went to graduate school. I might tell my friends and family that I was pursuing the PhD, but until I'd passed this barrier, Yale officially considered that I wasn't a degree candidate. Gossip abounded about graduate students from earlier classes who had deserved to pass but had been failed by vindictive faculty members. My class had "quals" at the end of the second year of study; I was worried along with every other student taking these examinations. We had begun with about nine men and eight women, but by this time one woman had said she just didn't care enough about biology and had dropped out. Each of us was individualistic, but for the purposes of this examination we had taken the same courses, reviewed the same materials, helped each other review, felt like cloned minds. We also had matching dark circles beneath our eyes from stress and late studying bouts. I smoked then, and had progressed to lighting one cigarette from the stub of the one before, existing in my own cloud of pollution.

The examinations had two parts. The professors gave us the written part first. They explained that after you passed the written part, you could schedule your oral examination. In Biology, the written examination was based on your chosen three core areas. Mine were genetics, biochemistry, and developmental biology. To me, these three looked like a continuum of DNA action. The genetics talked about how the DNA was passed on to the next generation, the biochemistry talked about how DNA made proteins and what proteins did, and the developmental biology talked about how the DNA was turned on at the right time in embryos. All DNA to me.

We waited for the written part of the quals to be handed to us, chatting nervously in corners about our degree of preparation. We were tough, sure, but this was the moment to decide our future. Could we do what we had planned? It was in the hands of those grading a subjectively-scored test. Between cigarettes, I bit off fingernails absentmindedly as I considered the consequences if I failed. Two of the men tried to play mind games, mentioning arcane findings in an offhand way that implied everyone should have them memorized. Cold sweat trickled down my back under the blue button-down Oxford-cloth shirt I wore.

The examination was in essay format. Each faculty member contributed questions covering his area. We were to answer all of the questions in the allotted time. The two professors administering the examination brought us into a medium sized seminar room and reminded us that no written materials were permitted. One candidate brought a purple pen, another brought a packet of about 100 pencils and pens from which to choose. I brought a blue pen and a black pen, and felt sorry I hadn't brought two of the same color so that no one could tell if my ink ran out. I toyed with a switch of my pony tail as I waited to get my paper with the test questions.

Everyone had official Yale blue books. From time to time during the test, someone groaned as he or she opened a new question and found the unexpected and unwelcome. We wrote in our blue books at great length. As directed in every one of the questions, we cited experimental papers wherever possible. My favorite question to answer was about the ribosome, a cell factory for making proteins. The question asked where it came from and how it was assembled. I had read quite a lot about this question and enjoyed organizing what I had learned.

My examinations at Goucher College had been in similar format, and I felt relatively comfortable. They hadn't asked me anything I couldn't write on. But not everyone had that reaction. Some of my women friends worried that they hadn't studied the right things; two said they had left a question blank.

Waiting to find out our grades was excruciating. A graduate student overheard one faculty member say to another, "Liz is such a weak student, we need to fail her on this test for the good of our program." (I've changed the names of the students in the paragraphs about this incident to protect the privacy of those concerned). This story spread rapidly over the graduate student grapevine. Liz heard this rumor and felt terrible. But the tests were anonymous during the grading. When the grades came out, there was only one person who didn't pass, and it was not Liz but Irene. We all thought they had guessed wrong about Liz's test and flunked Irene by mistake.

The other women students and I felt threatened by the implication that the professors were against us. How could they plot to flunk a woman when it was so hard to get women into science? They'd only do it if they didn't want us there. They were just pretending to accept women graduate students, to please someone higher up in the Yale administration. It never occurred to us at the time that the very stress of the examination could have caused someone to freeze during the test. We would have dismissed any thought that any of us wasn't ready. We talked about all this biology together so many times. We knew we all knew it.

I had passed, and passed well. Several faculty members told me that they had waited for the tests to be decoded to find out who had written the answers I gave, because they were so good. That was the written part. The orals were yet to come. I scheduled my oral examination several months ahead and I studied a little. I didn't prepare thoroughly for the orals because they were on genetics alone. I had been doing genetics for four years at Goucher, in summers at Woods Hole and Columbia University, and at Yale for two years. I felt like a golden child of genetics, one who knew it inside and out.

Norman Giles, the Southern gentleman whose laboratory group I had joined, would normally have chaired my oral examination. But he had left for his sabbatical leave in Australia. Bruce Carlton, a junior professor studying bacterial genetics, was in charge. Two weeks beforehand, he invited Peter Day to sit in on my oral examination, knowing that Peter Day had coauthored a famous book on fungal genetics. After all, he thought I was an aspiring fungal geneticist, planning to work with Norman Giles.

The committee called me into the bright, shabby seminar room on the second floor of Gibbs Laboratory to start my examination. They seated themselves around the table, leaving me standing with chalk in hand, ready for their questions. The first question was from tall, slender Peter Day. In his refined British accent, he asked, "Would you please diagram the life cycle of the fungus *Sordaria*?" My life didn't flash before my eyes. What did flash by my eyes: many diagrams showing life cycles for every known fungus; drawings that I had hastily thumbed past, to get to the interesting part of Fincham and Day's book.

"I'm sorry, but I can't do that," I said.

"Oh?" Peter Day said. "Well, what about the life cycle of *Coprinus*?"

"No, not that one either." I was shaking by then, so I sat down. How many fungal life cycles was he going to make me admit I didn't know? The answer was three more. By that time, I wouldn't have been able to tell him my name, had he asked me. He had thoroughly intimidated me and my mind had lost its ability to understand questions.

Bruce Carlton pushed his unruly lock of dark hair back from his forehead impatiently. He jumped in with a question he probably considered a nice low ball that I could hit out of the park. He dictated a problem about genetic crosses of mutants of bacterial viruses. I didn't solve it with any elegance or skill, but I muddled through.

He then asked, "What would you call that problem?"

My mind was blank; I was sure that I had already flunked the examination and couldn't focus on the question. He had asked me to name a three point cross, one of the two or three most common types of genetics problems. Normally I would have found his question simple.

"Maybe it's a three-point cross?" I said hesitantly.

They didn't ask any more, but just told me to go to my office. After five minutes, Bruce Carlton arrived there.

"What in the world was the matter with you?" he asked. "We couldn't believe you didn't seem to know anything. Of course you didn't pass. None of us understand it at all. You've worked so many genetics problems before."

I had nothing to say. I wondered if my career in science was over. After he stared at me for a minute, he left me sitting at my desk, looking vacant. I felt spacey and disconnected, almost as if I had been taking drugs. Why hadn't I studied those fungal life cycles? I probably thought they weren't all that important. I certainly wasn't interested in them. I never meant to spend my career studying fungi, although it would probably start that way. I had learned a lot about genetics in somatic human and mouse cells and in bacteria and viruses. No one had asked me if being an expert in fungal genetics was my career goal. Eventually, I stopped thinking and just sat there, stunned. No one came into the office. After a while I went home, cooked myself a bowl of mushroom soup, and went to bed. I couldn't get warm, so I kept getting more blankets.

The next day, Mary Case came to my office to say Giles had called. He had asked her to tell me I would have another oral examination when he returned from Australia. He said I should not worry.

I drew one wrong conclusion from that examination. I decided I couldn't be a professor. Students ask a professor unexpected questions and the professor has to answer them in real time. That was not something I was ever going to do again willingly.

I drew one right conclusion. I decided that the next time, I should over-study. I outlined the major ideas of genetics, including life cycles of every known fungus, and by the time of my next oral examination I knew them inside out. I could work the most arcane genetics problems. Since almost all known organisms made new gene combinations during sexual cell division or meiosis, I practiced genetics problems on those processes. But I also practiced problems about the exceptional types that mixed up their genes during non-sexual cell division or mitosis. I made sure I knew the gene exchange mechanisms in every type of odd-ball organism about which geneticists had published in the last twenty years. I could name every British investigator ever to study a gene and pronounce them correctly too, even Kacser (that's "catcher").

When the time came for the second try, I was nervous. I would surely be asked to leave if I failed again. The woman who had failed the written test was already gone. I loved DNA too much to let the system defeat me. Just this once I would speak and answer the questions. If I passed, I told myself I could go back to the lab for the rest of my career and be silent.

The Giles group had moved into Kline Biology Tower between my two oral exams. Giles came to my new office to get me. As he ushered me into the examination room he said, in a tone easily heard by all the examiners, "Let's get this mere formality over with." That moment is my favorite memory of Giles. Had he been a less formal man, had the stakes not been so high, in a different world, I would have kissed him for that sentence. It made me relax for a minute; it made me feel that he was sure I would pass and had no idea how I had ever failed the first time.

In the examining room, I felt like a robot running a well-rehearsed program with no bugs. Nothing fazed me. They asked me easy questions first. When I answered correctly, they went on to very difficult ones. I didn't have trouble with anything. But I couldn't smile. My zombie-self seriously explained everything. It was all flawless. I'm sure I spoke in a monotone with little expression, but only right answers were required, not presentation skills. When I left, I was sure I had passed.

I had proved to the examiners that I knew genetics. Far more significantly, I had proved it to myself. I was no "morning glory," receiving "Honors" grades in classes but never able to put it all together and complete the PhD. I was accepted, passed through the curtain of fire. Years later, I wished that the "I can't answer questions in public" baggage had burned along with my doubts about my genetics knowledge. But the possibility of being a professor didn't totally disappear from my mind and heart. It remained in suspended animation in my mental freezer until the time came to resurrect it.

Giles came to congratulate me, shook hands, and said, "And now down to the real work of a PhD, the dissertation research!" Once the pressure was off, my frozen state evaporated and I was elated, as if I were a champagne bottle whose cork had popped. I invited my office mates and everyone else I saw to George and Harry's, where we drank a huge amount of beer and wine at my expense, toasted all the arcane geneticists I could think of, and danced a hora. We sang biology songs I recalled from Woods Hole and Goucher, and I learned Tom Lehrer songs that friends had picked up at Harvard.

I had a horrible hangover the next morning, and didn't get up at all. I dragged myself into the lab around 2 PM and enjoyed

Turkish coffee with my friend and fellow graduate student Phil. I spent all afternoon being effusive about having passed, to the point that Phil threatened to let the rattlesnake out of his file cabinet if I didn't shut up. That evening, some of my friends took me out to Blessings Chinese Restaurant and we shared a Mongolian Hotpot, dipping our meat and vegetables into a communal bubbling broth that we drank at the end of the meal, and talking a mile a minute. Finally the euphoria wore off. I had passed. Now, I had to find a dissertation project.

CHAPTER 7
GRADUATE SCHOOL RESEARCH

Norman Giles wanted me to come to Yale and work with him on his project, and even undertook some administrative rearrangements to make it possible for Yale to readmit me when my proposed advisor at UCSD passed away. I am sure he acted partly because my senior thesis was on aromatic mutants. The Giles laboratory had recently begun a major project using these mutants. The genes called "arom" encoded proteins that stuck together to form a giant "enzyme complex," one that worked together to make the aromatic amino acids. The friendly interactions of the arom proteins increased their efficiency. Imagine a car factory where the chassis is assembled and passed to the next station in line where the door is added. Then the door location passes it on down the line to the windshield stop, and so forth. In the same way, the aromatic amino acids were assembled by proteins that were organized in an assembly line, passing the compounds from one to the next. Just drifting around in the cell waiting to run into the protein that could cause next step in the pathway was not efficient. But sticking the assembly together, so that the product of one reaction was passed to the site for the next reaction, streamlined the process and made it much faster. My familiarity with the aromatic mutant system could have been a leg up on my work on Giles' beloved new project.

When I got to Yale, I was to take courses and think about a project for about two years, but I received a desk in Norman Giles' research area. I went to the group seminars and felt like a bona fide member of the group from the start. Giles' group included three students who had already worked on the aromatic mutants or would do so, plus several postdoctoral fellows, Mary Case, the long term research associate of Norman Giles, and wild card graduate student Lorraine. She was a California girl.

I'd dreamed of becoming a California girl when I'd applied for graduate school at UCSD in La Jolla. Lorraine was blonde, long legged, and tan; she looked the part. But Lorraine wasn't in the lab day and night working on her project and she wasn't neat; these two qualities put her in Giles' persona non grata category. According to the dichotomy proposed by Francois Jacob in his autobiographical book The Statue Within, most of us in Giles' lab were "day scientists", working very logically and methodically with complicated prior planning and controls for each step. Lorraine was a "night scientist", hooked on creativity, less organized in her work habits and scientific experiment planning, but often onto something exciting.

Definitely, what Lorraine had was creativity. I never heard this from her, but she had a publication from her undergraduate days at UCLA on mating of *Paramecium*, a complicated microbe that many of us had to sketch in high school, badly in most cases. Her paper was published in the most prestigious journal at that time, *Proceedings of the National Academy of Sciences*. To do that work, she had to imagine that these microbes had four different sexes or mating types. That insight proved to explain a genetic system that had puzzled others for years. What was obvious to anyone who talked science with Lorraine was that she thought outside of the box. At this point in her graduate study, she wanted to know how genes caused shape changes.

Lorraine said to me, "I don't want to see a little machine

inside cells. I want to know why the whole thing looks the way it does. We have known about all of these mutants that cause shape changes for years, but nobody has ever found out how they work."

Her project had to do with a mutant called *fluffy* that made the pink bread mold look different; it was white and fuzzy because it didn't produce the conidia, the microscopic pink ball-shaped structures that normally coat the outside surface of the mold. She wanted to understand what caused the normal shape to form in the wild type, but a less complex shape to form in her mutant. "Don't be secretive, *fluffy*, spill it. What's up inside to make you look so different?"

I found Lorraine's question far more compelling than Giles'. Giles made a breakthrough that would show cooperation of the little units inside cells; I didn't see how important that finding would be. In a sense, Giles had mounted a micro scale challenge to nature-red-in-tooth-and-claw; his experiments would show that working together really produces better results. But I missed the significance of his ideas.

Early in my graduate study, I had told Bruce Carlton, Giles' protégé and junior colleague down the hall, that I would characterize his tryptophan mutants of the bacterium *Bacillus subtilis*. I kept going to his lab and trying to get started, but being told that there was no medium, no one had time to tell me how to make any, the mutants were frozen away and would have to be revived, etc. I enjoyed talking with his postdoc, Herb Boyer. The message from the others in the lab was subtle, but not encouraging. They didn't say anything straight out, but I couldn't make progress towards doing experiments there. The end of the idea of working on Carlton's project came on the day when Carlton met with me to tell me the background information. At our session, he made a number of disparaging remarks about a woman who had worked on these strains for her PhD elsewhere. I liked Carlton, and ended up valuing his input to my own thesis, but I suddenly didn't feel like I wanted to have him as primary advisor. What if he were to take against me in the same way? Those thoughts were never in the forefront of my mind, but today, mulling over why I stopped working on that project, they came to mind immediately. Now I also think it's possible that he saw me as Giles' student and tried not to steal me away.

I started reading *Neurospora Newsletter*, a periodical that was a written "chat room" for people working on genetics of Giles' favorite fungus. It had genetic maps, lists of mutants, and little notes from people who had invented a new method or produced a detailed genetic map. In there, I ran across mutants that I thought might be affecting the cell membrane. One was a potassium transport mutant, another was called 'osmotic' and couldn't grow on high salt concentrations. I found out from a new professor in Yale School of Medicine, Carolyn Slayman, who had discovered the potassium transport mutants, that they didn't have any shape difference. But I read in the newsletter that the osmotic ones did have a distinct and different shape. With the osmotic mutants, I thought there was a potential to connect a membrane mutation to a cell wall difference. I read more about them, and decided to propose the characterization of these mutants at the biochemical level to Giles as a thesis problem.

Not being very perceptive at that time, I didn't consider that Giles might not be happy with my choice. I wrote up the plan and made an appointment to present it to him. The day of the presentation, we sat down in his office, avoiding the sun from his large windows, and he said, "Well, what have you decided?"

"I would like to characterize the osmotic mutants," I said.

His face went from happy to wooden instantly. He didn't say anything for a minute.

"Why don't you tell me about it?"

I went through the reasons why it would be exciting to unveil the basis of a shape change, trying not to quote Lorraine. Then, I went on to describe the known characteristics of the osmotic mutants and what I wanted to do to find out what was wrong with them. I thought it likely that the cell wall, the entire outside layer of each cell, was assembled slightly wrong compared to wild type. I should be able to sort the mutants into genes by complementation tests, then I'd find the biochemical differences by analyzing the components of the wall and check on assembly problems by examining the cell wall's appearance in the electron microscope.

Giles said, "Let me think about it and get back to you Monday."

I went back to my office, feeling slightly chilled but not understanding why. A postdoctoral fellow with whom I had shared an office earlier, Liz, was there planning an experiment on my blackboard, in a delicious cloud of lemony Jean Nate perfume. She asked how things were going. I told her what had just happened, and she told me Giles was probably unhappy about my not choosing his area to work in.

"But wouldn't he want me to be creative in choosing a problem, and take what might have the best payoff long term?" I asked.

"He's more a researcher than a teacher," Liz replied. She was probably right, I thought. He would glory in his lab's current achievements before he would push a student out to the edge of knowledge. But I was ignoring the fact that his project was also at the edge of knowledge. It just wasn't the problem I had chosen, I didn't feel connected to it. To me, ownership was a major issue. I wanted to work on what really moved me. I wanted to discover something about shape regulation. Demanding my own problem was the first place that I made a stand scientifically and I'm still drawing that line in the sand, not working on the "in" problems, but working on questions I find compelling.

Giles agreed that I could work on osmotic mutants, and I

settled in to do genetic screens for mutants and to characterize the osmotic mutants that I collected. After about two years of constant research, I had identified the genes by complementation, then showed that each of the types of osmotic mutants had a different kind of cell wall. I felt that my research was nearing its end when Giles told me that my dissertation committee wanted a summary of my results. I delivered it to him and awaited their reaction.

He approached me down the hall and stopped to say, "Laurie, the committee isn't ready to recommend that you be graduated. They want more experiments on certain issues." He said he would give me a list of their requirements the next day.

I went back to my office and sat down. I felt like the rug had been pulled out from under me. I was almost through. How could they say I needed more experiments? I had done almost one hundred amino acid analyses of the cell walls from these mutants, cell wall carbohydrate analyses, lipid analyses, and electron micrographs of cell walls.

By that time Lorraine had completed her degree and gone, and I remembered that something like this had happened at the end of her thesis too. Was this a special treat for women, to get an ultimatum for more work when they thought they should be able to leave? Or had we simply not thought through what would be necessary to convince the world of our findings? Today, I can see that our lack of contact with Giles produced the demand at the end that seemed so unreasonable back then. We should have shown our results to Giles often; barging in with them if necessary. Because we didn't, the final demands were probably inevitable. He was our dissertation advisor, the quality control monitor for our thesis work. He had to make sure it was done right, and we had kept it all secret from him for most of the process.

That was the big difference between how Lorraine and I operated and how the men did. They were all free and easy with Giles. I had broken that relationship by not picking a problem in his area of research, and it was never really repaired. I can't recall one time when he had asked to see my data or I had offered to show it to him. It didn't occur to me how atypical that was for him. I just thought it was because I wasn't working on his thing. True, but I was still his student. Now I had to wait for the news of what remained to be done, sunk into the worry well.

In the interim, what kept me sane was the thought that I was almost finished with a project that connected DNA with its effects. Those genes made a big difference in the biochemistry of the cell wall, in the shape and appearance of the mutants, and in their ability to resist high concentrations of salt. I felt I was unveiling DNA's mysteries, and I could see about two scientific papers' worth of strong data in my completed work. I felt like no last-minute barriers could take away my feeling of accomplishment.

CHAPTER 8
LET ME OUT OF HERE

Giles said, "Here is our list of what you still need to complete." His voice was flat, final; he couldn't meet my eyes. The list was folded over.

I looked at him for a second, then took the list and walked around our floor in the Kline Biology Tower to my office. I had six weeks of NSF Graduate Fellowship funding left to complete my PhD work, finish writing my dissertation, and have an oral defense with my degree committee. My lease ran out in six weeks too. I sat down shakily and unfolded the list.

Item number one would take at least two months to complete. It said, "Cross mutant at putative new locus to the linkage tester strain and determine linkage group." Let me explain what they wanted me to do. We had a fungus strain in the laboratory, the "linkage tester strain" that had mutations at known sites along each one of the chromosomes. If you crossed an unknown mutant with this tester and examined the offspring, you could tell where your gene was located (its "linkage") by the combinations of known genes with your new mutant gene among those offspring.

Genetic crosses were slow. I sat and stared at the list, wondering what was going to happen to me. Would I have to stay at Yale forever? Where would I stay? How would I eat? Would I be sent home to North Carolina in disgrace, to work at K Mart and talk about my almost-PhD?

My office mate, Karim, came in and said, "What did they demand?" He knew all about the coming of the list; we had discussed it and he was very sympathetic.

"I have to cross with the linkage tester." He knew immediately that the genetic cross I had been asked to complete was arduous and time consuming.

"Oh, no, that's really awful. Can I help?"

"Karim, I really appreciate it, but the time it takes is all in the setting up of the cross; the analysis isn't bad. But I'm sure I can't finish it in the time I thought I had left."

"What about your postdoc?" Karim asked.

I had set up a postdoctoral fellowship with Frank Young at Scripps Clinic and Research Foundation in La Jolla, California. There, I planned to work on bacteria with mutations affecting the structure of their cell walls. It would continue some themes from my dissertation in a new organism. It was supposed to start in six weeks. I hadn't even thought about that yet.

"I will have to let Frank know and see if I can come later. At least I have an NIH Postdoctoral Fellowship so he won't have money hanging fire in the deal. I hope he will not mind."

"He probably won't care."

My brain was swooping with worry about starting the experiment, finding money to pay for food and housing, the time the experiment might take. Luckily, all of the other experiments on the list could easily be completed while the cross was taking place. I didn't ask myself, "What if the cross fails?"

Somehow, I put the housing and food in the back of my mind and set to work on the experiments. My friend Lois, who had dropped out of the Yale graduate program by that point, had once told me that to get a PhD you needed to fail a personality test. You needed to agree you would only see science. At that moment, I felt she was right. All else but that list was squeegeed from my life and the bright focus on science blinded me to any other concerns, even worrying about where I was going to stay and how I was going to eat.

When I had two weeks left on my lease and was two weeks into burning up the money from my last stipend check, Mary Case pulled me aside as I was going down the hall.

"Where are you staying?" she asked.

"I have my apartment for two more weeks, but then I don't know," I said, suddenly recalling that I had developed no options.

Mary, perhaps pitying me and perhaps as a favor for her old friend Ann Lacy, my Goucher advisor, said, "You can stay at my place for a month, and I will feed you dinners." Mary had a beautiful two-bedroom apartment furnished with Danish teak furniture and she was a gourmet cook, although she probably weighed in at 110 pounds on her five-feet-seven frame.

I suddenly felt that my life was more possible. I would survive this after all. "Mary, you're blessing," I said with a big smile.

"No problem," she said, ducking her head in embarrassment.

The cross with the infamous linkage tester strain and my new mutant type was finally set up, the spores were isolated and "cooking" and I had completed the rest of the experiments and all of the writing. It was Sunday afternoon, and I'd come into the laboratory to test the outcome of the cross. I opened the incubator and picked up the rack with the many tubes containing the isolated individual offspring. I grabbed several racks of tester medium test tubes and sat down with a large pad to record the plans for testing the offspring. But where were they? Each of these test tubes was supposed to have a nice little mold, resulting from my cross. I would then fill in their number and what media I was going to test them on, and start the growth experiments. Most of the tubes were empty. No germination of the spores I had carefully picked and placed into those tubes. Oops, there was one, and there was another one, but so few. How could I test for the genetic linkage when almost none of the offspring had grown?

One of my beloved father's stories came to my mind to tempt me. He had told me about an experiment he was required to complete when working on his Masters degree in chemical engineering at Ole Miss. When sucrose breaks down into two smaller sugars, the optical rotation of light changes. My Dad tried to get this well known result, but never could. He told me he had never really understood why this should happen and he had never been able to observe it either. He had just made up his data so he could go on and finish the degree. I had agonized over this story before, wanting to admire my Dad but feeling that he had made a shameful choice. So here I was, facing disaster. Would I make the same choice as my Dad?

I sat at the table a long time with my stomach churning. Finally, I decided to analyze those few progeny I had, and hope that I could decipher the map from them. So, I made a pitifully short list of them on my cross-hatched paper and set them gently on the top layers of several different kinds of test growth media. I was almost nuts with worry about what the results would be. But there was nothing I could do about it. I had to wait until the progeny gave me their answer; two days of hell.

Luckily one of Giles' graduate students from two classes behind my own, a Texas charmer called Kent Keeton, decided to distract me from my problems. He said we should visit Giles' secretary Connie Payne in her other life. By night, Connie worked at the Cotton Club, a black night club about six blocks away, up the street from the Yale Coop store. So we went there and had a very relaxing time. When the musicians were taking a break, they played recordings of Otis Redding, so I got to know and love his music before his mega-hit "Dock of the Bay" put him on everyone's screen.

Connie was a husky black woman about six feet tall, very

feminine. She nicknamed everyone. I'm sorry to say my nickname was "Mess". I often asked her to do complicated things for me, in part due to a lack of planning ahead. But I guess my nickname is better than my friend Bob's. He first visited her office wearing *lederhosen*, so he was dubbed "Hotpants" forever after. Connie called my office mate, Karim El Eryani, "Ery". One day I was surprised to see Karim bringing a crowd of six male Arabic students down the hall with him. They were giggling and snickering. He brought them to Connie's office.

She said, "Hi Ery, how are you doing?" Every one of those men convulsed with laughter and practically fell on the ground foaming at the mouth. Connie looked at them in puzzlement, shrugged, and went back to her typing. Later Karim revealed to her that Ery means "my penis" in Arabic. She thought it was a good joke too.

After two days of trying to distract my mind in whatever ways I could, I came back to score the few progeny from that cross I was required to complete. I took all the racks to my desk and sat there with the short list of progeny, recording their phenotypes. When I was done, I tried to make a map. The sun was shining in my office window on my Indian rug, highlighting the purple and red *Coleus* foliage plant in the window that had gone to seed due to my neglect. It was hard for me to concentrate on these calculations. Obviously I didn't have enough data to be definitive. The analysis wasn't great, but it worked after a fashion; I made a map. The replication was really poor, but I hoped the committee would accept it.

Today, I'd like to go back and do the cross over. Then, I felt that I had a large body of work to present and this was only a detail. What I could have learned, if I had been more open to it, was the importance of approaching a conclusion by more than one line of experiment. I had to learn that lesson during my postdoctoral training instead. Now, I help college seniors to incorporate multiple approaches into their senior theses. It's much more convincing when you've supported the conclusion with different kinds of evidence.

I went in to present the results to Giles, and he looked at them for a long time in silence, and then said, "I guess this will have to do." I was deliriously happy to hear that at the time. The reverberation I can hear now is that he wasn't proud of me, and had little confidence that my results were robust. In fact, the map turned out to be wrong. Two years later, when I attended a meeting of people working on *Neurospora*, a Stanford professor took me aside and told me that the map I had drawn was wrong and couldn't be repeated.

He said, "I looked at your data and they're pretty scanty. Actually they're consistent with the real map, within experimental error." I knew I had marginal genetic data for that map. Was I the victim of my own bad decision making in planning my thesis work to begin with? Or, had I just done what I had to do, completed the degree, and then gone on to bigger and better things? Had I been subjected to another trial of fire reserved for women only, the last-minute-data-demand? If so, whose fault was it? Mine because I never dropped in to talk with Giles? His because he never gave me any reason to think he might be interested in my results? In any case, I had done something less than my best. But, I hadn't actually made up data, so I clung to that thought and got on with my life.

CHAPTER 9
THE TWO BODY PROBLEM

In 1968, after the generosity of Mary Case had rescued me from the ignomy of running out of money before completing my PhD, I went to Scripps Clinic and Research Foundation in La Jolla, California to begin a postdoctoral fellowship. With the encouragement of my new mentor, Frank Young, I had applied for and obtained a two year National Institutes of Health (NIH) postdoctoral fellowship. I was excited about this opportunity, because Frank and his colleagues had discovered how bacteria can defeat the viruses that want to infect and kill them. The bacteria simply eliminate a rococo handle on their cell walls to which the viruses attach, so they become resistant to infection. The cell-wall-handle probably had another function that was lost in these mutants, but the bacteria seemed to grow fine without it. Probably it was helpful but not essential. Making bacteria resist virus attacks by mutation was the kind of experiment that I had found fascinating even during introductory biology at Goucher. My Goucher friend Terry, whose research interests were generally far from mine, had heard of these experiments of Frank's. When I told her I wanted to go to his lab for a postdoc, she said that his experiments were very well designed.

I have always enjoyed scientists who can sell their ideas. Frank Young was the kind of a guy who went to the American

Heart Association and gave such a good talk that they fawned on him and fell all over themselves to give him funds, although he didn't work on anything that was remotely connected to heart disease. He could have had a great career as a patent medicine pitch man. But instead, he became an MD and a scientist. After my stint in his lab, he moved on from Scripps Clinic and Research Foundation to become the director of the Federal Drug Agency, running the drug safety programs for the whole country.

When I arrived in his laboratory, Frank introduced me to the crew. His senior postdoctoral fellow was Dale, and he also had Willie, Paul, and me as postdoctoral researchers, and Skip for a graduate student. His technicians included Luciano, Pat, and Cary. So, here was a first rate, renowned science group in 1968 with two white males, a black male, and a white female as postdocs, a white male grad student, and a Latino and two women as technicians. I felt like I was in the garden of diversity, and wondered if it there would be tensions and conflicts beyond what I had seen in graduate school. I thought it was exciting, though, and I liked all the people in the laboratory. In fact, no race or gender-based conflicts developed while I was there. That helped me get over any concerns about working in groups of diverse scientists.

In retrospect, I have chewed over why I didn't expect to get a faculty appointment coming out of graduate school. In those days, postdoctoral fellowships were optional for people with very strong degrees who didn't plan to switch fields. Most of my male colleagues from Yale had gone directly into faculty positions, while the females had been directed to postdoctoral positions. I hadn't yet realized the trend in what had happened, so I was a sleeping feminist, not yet awakened. My rhinoceros mental skin was protecting me from insights that I was accumulating. I sorted and mulled over those experiences later in my life.

Back then, I didn't have the 'voice' of a professor. I hadn't spoken up much at all in college, unless called upon. In graduate school, I had just started to come out of my shell when I failed the oral examination. At that point, I was convinced I didn't have what it took to become a professor. After I survived the second oral quals, I tried to become a bit more vocal, but I didn't have a relaxed, conversational style.

Ironically, at that time I had more of a political and social voice than I've had subsequently. People thought I was brash and presumptuous. I was elected president of the biology graduate students and felt I had to fight for the graduate students' lounge. Some of the professors wanted to use it as a classroom or a library. I met with professors and argued forcefully for keeping it purely for relaxation. I also tried to get the Biology Chair to make the bathrooms in Kline Biology Tower unisex, since there was only one on each floor. He finally told me that if I wanted a degree, I should drop the issue.

I went with one of my friends to try to convince the Dean of Yale Graduate School that the university should not build more graduate dorms, separating the students from the city. We argued that Yale should partner with the city to build affordable apartments. The Dean was very polite to us though he paid us no heed. I spoke up when I cared about issues, but speaking in public wasn't a joy to me at all then. I probably didn't put the "speaking up" in the same category as science talks.

The Giles group had Jerry as a model for a graduate student destined to be a professor. We all had to make presentations to a weekly Journal Club, explaining a new article from the literature when it was our turn. Jerry was always smooth and articulate and never sounded abrasive. His presentations were highly organized. He reviewed the background, and took us to the forefront of innovation. On the other hand, I always finished my presentations early. I assumed I didn't have to explain the background, since at that time I was convinced that the audience knew it all before I started speaking.

I had to be assertive to get any experience teaching Yale undergraduates. I begged every semester to teach a class. Since my NSF Graduate Fellowship fully funded both my tuition and my stipend, they always said I didn't "need" the money. I felt I did need the experience.

Although my mental image of me as a professor was frozen away at the bottom of my mind, subconsciously I was working towards that goal. The biologists finally let me be the Teaching Assistant for Norman Giles' genetics laboratory once, at the end of my third year. I met with two laboratory sections when they did their experiments, had a tutorial session with the students in my labs to discuss course material, and graded all of their genetics homework problems. I really enjoyed it and I felt like I did a good job; however, I didn't see it as real teaching. To me, teaching meant lecturing, answering questions, giving and grading examinations. Here, I didn't have to deliver lectures (except 15 minute laboratory talks) or grade examinations. I wasn't getting those killer questions from the students that called forth my "deer in the headlights" response, the response I'd given to the fungal life cycle questions on my first oral examination. Even when I presented journal clubs, which were more like the lectures I felt I couldn't give, I didn't make much eye contact and wrote little on the board. Talking in public about science had been a trial since I'd failed the oral examination, and although I don't remember formally deciding, I probably thought I would be better off going for a research career.

Now I was starting a postdoctoral fellowship at a purely research institution, so I felt that I wouldn't need to give public talks or teach much at all. La Jolla was as beautiful as I remembered it. For some time, I had kept a poster on my office door at Yale saying "La Jolla is a way of life" and showing a photograph of a beach. Once I arrived in La Jolla, I enjoyed running on the beach after work, constantly amazed at the turquoise-to dark blue shading of the water. I ran and walked several miles each day at sunset. Then I went home to a tiny house owned by the clinic, right next door. It had a huge dark red bougainvillea rambling over the back fence and the garage roof. Behind it, visible from my living room was the ocean, sometimes with visible spouting grey whales. I started dinner, sat and looked out the window as dusk fell, drank a glass of Fume Blanc or Chardonnay, and thought all was right with the world.

The one thing that preyed on my mind was a fear of tidal waves; after all we were right at the beach. The idea seems silly in retrospect, but I was concerned, so I bought a life jacket and kept it under my desk. Skip and Paul thought this was the craziest thing they had ever seen, and constantly teased me about it. Finally one day, as I was sitting at my desk reading an article, the cabinet next to me began to chatter and I wondered if we were having an earthquake. Then a small glob of water hit my journal. I looked up to see an empty cup on the top of my bookcase, dripping its final drop onto my article. Then I noticed the fishing line connecting the cabinet to the work bay behind me. A fishing line also ran from the empty cup back that way. When I rounded the corner to see what was up over there, I found two convulsed men, practically rolling on the floor with laughter. "We got you going, didn't we?" Skip was finally able to squeeze out between bouts of laughter. He did indeed. I went to the library and read about tidal waves, finding that the deep water just off our shore meant a tidal wave had no chance to reach towering heights. I quietly took home my life jacket and put it to good use later on deep sea fishing trips.

My new laboratory's research was about the cell surfaces of *Bacillus subtilis*, a common type of bacteria. I began to study how a sugar called glucose was added to the cell wall at specific places, making the bacteria susceptible to infection by a virus. I wanted to study TAG Transferase, an enzyme (the type of protein that speeds up a reaction). The TAG Transferase's job was to attach the sugar to the cell wall. My protein was located in the cell membrane. To study it, I needed to detach it, because all of the ways to study enzymes require that the enzyme be dissolved, not stuck on something.

The laboratory next door was run by a specialist in "chaotropic ion extraction," a method to remove proteins from membranes. His method used charged groups or ions that caused chaos in the arrangement of water molecules. When the water got disordered, the nice, neat "oil-water" separation of the membrane broke down and proteins could escape from the membrane. He taught me this method, and I found it would work for my enzyme. Once I got it out of the membrane, along with a mixture of unwanted proteins, the next job was to purify it using separation columns and then characterize it.

That part of my research involved hours of standing at the spectrophotometer in front of the big windows looking out at the ocean. There I could watch whales spouting, dolphins jumping, and fishing boats baking in the sun as I determined how much protein and how much enzyme activity were in each numbered tube from my column separations.

My social skills were still underdeveloped, but I had a good friend, Sue Bonner, who was a technician in a laboratory down the hall, and who was emphatically an "interesting person." She and her husband Phil, a graduate student up at University of California, San Diego (UCSD) made my life at Scripps Clinic fun. We listened to recorded plays (including "Who's Afraid of Virginia Wolfe"), had silent meditations, and ate a lot of dinners together.

Once, Phil lent me his Aston Martin to go to a lecture up the hill at UCSD. I had driven a shift car before, but wasn't really all that comfortable with them, and I had never driven an Aston. There is a steep hill on Prospect Avenue in downtown La Jolla on the way to the university, and I ended up as the first car at a red light at the top of Prospect. I was having a hard time managing the brake and the clutch, so I put the emergency brake on. When the light changed, I couldn't figure out how to release it. I looked all around on the floor and the steering column, but nothing was there. Finally I had to get out the instruction manual, fortunately still in the glove compartment, and read the part about the emergency brake. Meanwhile, the ever-patient rich people of La Jolla had worn out their horns and exercised their "cursive" vocabulary well. I felt like Bill Cosby in San Francisco, beckoning and shouting, "Come around, come around!"

After I'd been working at Scripps Clinic awhile, I noticed a black man who dropped by to chat with Willie, the African American postdoc in our lab. His name was Richard, and he was always pleasant and upbeat. I asked Willie about him, and heard that he was the account manager and equipment purchasing advisor for one of the immunology superstars at Scripps and had come to La Jolla with him from Pittsburgh several years earlier. Richard told a funny story about beef rib barbeques on the beach, stocked with free beef ribs. His friend, "Cookie" the cook, had obtained the ribs as throwaways, because he worked in Bully's, a famous prime rib restaurant in La Jolla. He and Cookie had invited the restaurant owner to one of the barbecues, after which he stopped giving Cookie the ribs and put them on the menu!

Richard invited me to hear the Pittsburgh Symphony perform in downtown San Diego. He picked me up from my ocean-view mini-house and took me to his car, which was an ancient beast known as "the gray ghost." This car had a large hole in the floor on the passenger side, and he warned me not to step carelessly. It was unnerving to see the road rushing past under my feet. He told me he had bought the car from a poor, starving postdoc for $25. When he left La Jolla, he sold it to another poor postdoc for the same price. So, one of the first things I found out about Richard was that he hated to spend money. Or maybe, that he hated to spend money unnecessarily—he had bought symphony tickets, after all.

You might think that hell must have frozen over, for this Southern girl to go out with a black man. Back at Yale, I had not encouraged Marvin, my black friend who roomed in the same condemned apartments over George and Harry's bar in New Haven, but for some reason, Richard got under the radar. I didn't actually think about going out with him as a potential problem for some time, and when it hit me, it was too late.

We went out driving around the countryside, hiked on the desert trails, and visited the famous San Diego zoo. Once, we went with several friends on a hike to an oasis in the desert at Anza Borrego State Park. Of course it was terribly hot and dry, and you couldn't see the oasis, or much of anything else, on the horizon from our starting point. There was a trail we followed, though. It was the first hike I went on that had a frisson of terror associated with it. What would happen to us if we couldn't find the oasis and lost the trail? Lots of movies had made it clear that disaster was a likely outcome. After a three hour hike with many stops to sip from canteens, we arrived at the oasis. It was in a crease in the ground, and a small spring welled up among the dense palms surrounding the water. The palms completely obscured the water until we were very close to it, and these palms didn't look anything like the ones I had seen in La Jolla. I asked if they were a different species.

"Maybe," said my friend Sue, "But more likely, they just aren't trimmed up the way the city does them."

I looked more carefully and saw that she was right; the palms were shrouded in convoluted, extensive, burgeoning husk-like old leaf bases that are always trimmed off in cities, lest they break a window in high winds. The trunks were five feet across, palms with elephantiasis. An eerie aspect of the oasis was its silence. Richard said he hadn't heard so little noise ever before except when he was asleep. The oasis was also very dark, and that darkness was welcome after the terribly bright walk across the desert for several hours. We rested and drank, ate lunches, and then walked back across to the cars.

Richard and I talked in the car on the way to various events, so I began to find out about his life. I learned that he had been married; his former wife Margaret was his childhood sweetheart whom he had married while he was attending the University of Pittsburgh majoring in Political Science. He had gotten a part time job working in the laboratory of his immunology lab director, and eventually it had evolved into full time research. In those days, he had even been an author on presentations at FASEB, the meetings of forty or fifty thousand biomedical researchers, mostly held in Atlantic City back then. His lab director called him "Coeur" after Richard the Lion Hearted, and had given him a silver shot glass with this name engraved on it. He and Margaret had three kids, Greg and Reggie and then Pam, and they had moved out to San Diego with his supervisor, when he came to Scripps Clinic. Around that time, Richard had switched to supervising the purchase of major equipment items for his boss's very large and well funded research group, and he was doing little or no research when I met him.

The equipment salesmen wined and dined him when they came to town, and sometimes I was invited along. I recall one favorite salesman, Pete, who told us about when he was sent as a National Guardsman to guard the first black university students during early integration in the South.

"Those girls and guys," Pete said, "didn't do a thing to anybody, they just wanted to learn, and here these dirty-mouthed men and women were yelling obscenities and threats at them. Because they wanted to learn! It's enough to make you throw up."

Another time, I had a front row seat as Richard negotiated a great deal on an amino acid analyzer with a Japanese company trying to break into the US market. He negotiated for a while, and then said, "No, I like you people, but you guys don't really want to make a deal," as he got up to leave.

The representatives jumped up and urged him to sit down again, saying, "But yes, we do, we do," and they cut the price, offered free extra columns, free reagents, etc. In the end, the deal was so irresistible that the cagey investigators who were the main users of the equipment were stunned with the offer. They okayed it immediately. These same Japanese salesmen were still grateful to Richard for helping them get a foot in the door in the US, and when they next came by Scripps, they brought him a Pentax camera that was state of the art for its day.

Richard told me he was a Republican, "Party of Lincoln," he said. His whole family voted Republican, but went to the parties the Democrats held in Homewood, a Pittsburgh neighborhood near the University of Pittsburgh where his family lived.

"The dummies never even asked how we planned to vote," he said; "I guess they thought that since they were feeding us and giving us some booze, we would vote their way."

I didn't much like the Republican party, but I was worn out from working for Eugene McCarthy and trying to end the war by political activism in graduate school, so I didn't argue, but just told him I was a Democrat. "Too bad, I thought you were smart," he said, with a wicked grin.

One of the attractive things about Richard was that wicked grin. You couldn't help being drawn into an implied conspiracy with him when you saw it. He had an irresistible sense of humor, and he saw humor in situations that would have just made me angry. I wish I had learned that from him, but I never did. Years later, my kids would tell me, "Mom, you have no sense of humor." But he wasn't willing to set aside racial slurs with a joke. Willie told me that Richard had taken on an administrator at Scripps about how he was being treated and got proper respect from then on. He was friends with the other black people at Scripps, many of whom worked in the animal quarters. He told me about one man who always ended his conversations with Richard by saying, "Let's get a busload and wipe these honkies out!" Richard treated it as a joke, but I'm not sure the animal caretaker meant it that way.

I needed to learn a lot about black people's sensitivities while we were dating. Back during high school, my friend Jeanne had moved down to Charlotte with her family just before high school, and she was active in demonstrating at segregated lunch counters in Charlotte with the National Conference of Christians and Jews. I thought I would like to do that too, but I never actually did. I wish I could say that I was moved by the injustice of dime stores not serving black people, a major group of their customers. But, my recollection is that the excitement was what really attracted me. On the other hand, Jeanne told me that usually nothing happened; the owners would just close the lunch counter after the demonstrators sat there for an hour or two. She wasn't sure it was having any effect. But it seemed to me that the demonstrators had the upper hand; the owners surely got no money, their food was wasted, and the convenience the owners had hoped to provide for shoppers was vitiated.

In retrospect, I was right on that one, but very, very wrong on the big picture. I remember one late night conversation with Jeanne when I shocked her by saying that I was grateful to be white. I just didn't know what was wrong with that way of thinking at all. My mental armor, which functioned well for keeping me in science in spite of various negative signals, kept me from empathizing with others who were enduring situations that I clearly understood to be unacceptable.

In La Jolla, I didn't plan to cure the discrimination against black people by dating a black man. But I had found a man who wasn't cowed by my status as a PhD or a scientist, who could laugh with me or even at me from time to time, who was fun to be with, enjoyed many of the same things that I did, and lived comfortably in the same world I did.

Richard and I took his kids to a baseball game, the Padres against another team that I no longer remember. The kids were very polite and on their best behavior. Even so, I could see some of their individual personalities during the evening. Pam was mainly interested in the food and the musical selections; she bubbled over with enthusiasm about the music, but not the game. Reggie knew all the stats on every player on both teams, and had a serious look but a big smile when something exciting happened in the game. Greg had gravitas and wanted to talk with Richard about what he knew about engineering programs at various colleges; he was working at the Naval Engineering Laboratory each summer. I wondered if he was a genius; his mind was clearly profound.

Richard didn't want to buy the kids anything to eat or drink, saying, "Did we come to see baseball or to eat?" I talked him into cotton candy and cokes, at least.

On the way home, he told me that he would have no clothes and no car except for the fact that he knew how to squeeze a penny until it screamed for mercy.

He said, "I pay child support to Margaret, as I should. But, it makes me think a lot about each penny I spend; I don't have anything to waste, and I want to make sure I'm spending for things I really want, not just responding to ads." That made me worry about the amount he was suddenly spending on taking me places, although the nights out were mixed with free events like desert hikes. Why was spending on me such a high priority?

Well, I soon found out. He asked me to marry him. I probably should not have been as surprised as I was. I was even more surprised to hear myself saying yes. After the fact, I realized that marrying him was what I really wanted to do.

Then we had to tell the families. He didn't want to tell his family, and I didn't want to tell mine. I decided I had to do it. I called up and told my Mom; Dad wasn't home. She became very quiet and asked a few questions like. "What about kids?" She said she would talk with Dad and they would call me back.

I was afraid of that call. I needed to talk with someone before it came, so I tried to make an appointment with the pastor at the Presbyterian Church where Richard was a member. It was hard getting through his protective secretaries, but I finally succeeded. Richard agreed to go with me. The pastor seemed pleased with the news that we wanted to get married, and asked if we wanted to be married in the church. He told us that the Presbyterian Church had recently affirmed its willingness to perform marriage ceremonies for people of different races. Richard said that we planned to get married elsewhere but would like him to officiate. That was fine, but I was surprised to hear it. Later he told me that he had talked with one of our friends about getting married in her back yard.

Louis, the minister, then asked how our families felt about the marriage. We had to admit we hadn't told them much yet. He emphasized that a family is a life long commitment that can't really be repudiated. He added that last part since he saw Richard making a face. He told us how important it was to keep conversation going even in the face of a negative response. Family relationships were too valuable to let the bonds be disrupted, he felt. I agreed with him, but was still nervous about the upcoming conversation, and said so. I told him my family roots were in Mississippi and that this marriage wasn't welcome to my mom and dad. He urged me to try to emphasize Richard's good points, our compatibility, and any similarities I could think of to their situation when they married. That idea got me in a lot of trouble.

When we finally connected by phone, Mom said I should worry about a class difference between us, not just a racial difference. I responded that I thought in some sense Mom was from a higher social class than Dad, but that their marriage had worked out. Dad erupted, saying that I was completely wrong, they were from exactly the same social class. I know that the violent response was really more about my marriage plans, but I had evidently pushed a sensitive button. Now I had to backtrack and pacify him. So I said I had misunderstood and was sorry, but I didn't really think Richard's family were socially far below me either. Dead silence.

Then they brought up grandkids. What they apparently wanted was for me to say I wouldn't have kids. I didn't say that. They wanted grandkids, I suppose, but having black grandkids was another matter. But they never said that in so many words. Our conversation ended with a truce rather than a peace, but at least we were still talking. After four more rounds over the next month, they finally seemed to become resigned to the idea. Richard had called his family once and gotten a silent treatment. He wasn't able to discuss it at all, and he didn't keep trying either.

Meanwhile, Richard's lab director was negotiating with National Jewish Hospital in Denver to go there, bring in a large group, and hire others after he arrived. He arranged for Richard to become a hospital administrator in the main office there, which he thought would be a good step up for him. They moved to Denver while I was still in the midst of the first year of my two year postdoctoral fellowship, and we arranged to have our wedding in La Jolla right at the end of year one of my fellowship. I flew out to Denver and interviewed with various labs where I might want to transfer my fellowship for year two. I chose the lab of Ernest Borek at University of Colorado Medical School, only two blocks from National Jewish Hospital.

Richard flew back to La Jolla right before the wedding. My Mom and Dad came to the wedding but none of his relatives did. It was in our friend's back garden, and there were about 60 people there. Louis brought his wife and also a famous movie star, Marge Champion, who happened to be visiting him that day. Many of our friends from Scripps were there. I had made the music tapes at my friend Pat's house, while we watched the first moon walk by Neil Armstrong on TV. After the wedding, we had a great party and then went off on our honeymoon.

In spite of their acquiescence, my parents expected us to encounter opposition at every turn, but we didn't encounter it often, at least not overtly. Nothing untoward happened on our honeymoon, in which we drove up the California coast to Big Sur, and then wended our way across to Denver in the early October blizzard that year. We stayed for while in the apartment Richard had been renting, which was half a block from National Jewish and across the street from a junior high school whose running track we used for our workouts.

Soon, we moved to a new high-rise apartment building behind the University of Colorado Medical School, encountering no race problem in renting. We settled down to married life, and with the workouts, were able to lose some weight and go hiking in the mountains quite a bit. We had two of Richard's kids, Pam and Reggie, come visit, and then drove them back to San Diego, stopping at Mesa Verde and the Grand Canyon. A picture of Pam on that trip makes me sad, because her collar is sticking up. She asked me for an iron, but I didn't have one. It was part of my strategy not to type, not to iron, etc.

Richard and I led a normal life. Many of our friends had told us we could expect people to ostracize us; we could expect stares on the street. The only thing about our married life in Denver that was race-specific was our interactions with our families.

The career implications of getting married weren't quite as benign, though. I had moved from a good laboratory just as we started getting results, which was frustrating. We published a paper on TAG Transferase, partly because the postdoc who replaced me continued that line of experiments to completion. But publishing one paper in a field and then switching to a different research subject didn't look good on my Curriculum Vitae (what academics call the resume). It was lucky that even one paper was published though. I've known other women scientists who encountered the "two body problem" where one member of the couple, usually the man, moves and the other has to drop everything to go along, who were left with nothing after a year or two of hard work in the laboratory.

CHAPTER 10
BOREK'S WORLD

When Richard and I moved to from La Jolla to Colorado, I transferred my National Institutes of Health postdoctoral fellowship to the laboratory of Ernest Borek. Ernest had "retired" from City College of New York to University of Colorado Medical School, so he could ski. He had married his research associate Sylvia. The two of them bought a house in Denver and a second home in Breckinridge, once made famous by Jean-Claude Killy, a retired Olympic skier.

Ernest, a tall, husky man with bunches of wild black hair surrounding a big bald spot, said to me, "I'm a Hungarian and proud of it. You Americans don't know how to write, but I had to learn to write English the hard way and I have become a good writer. Not great but good. You guys should work at writing. It's the best skill a scientist can have. How will anyone ever hear about your work unless you write? And if you write badly, when they hear, they won't care!"

He organized work in the laboratory so that we worked through the weekends when ski lift lines were long and had off Monday and Tuesday when lift lines were short. Sometimes he drove us up to ski himself, bellowing Hungarian folk tunes all the way. A lot of the postdocs in his lab worked right through and never took any days off, working 15-20 hour days, week after week. I didn't ski much, so I was often in this group of workaholics.

In his group, Ernest had quite a few subordinate women. His group consisted of his wife Sylvia as a research associate, postdocs Rae, Margaret, Stan, Judy, Opendra, and me, and one graduate student, Rosemary. He also had Vera, a Bulgarian technician who mainly worked with Sylvia and Opendra, and Mary, an unskilled but nice lab helper. Borek said we worked under the sign of the methyl group. The methyl group is a small clump of atoms that can be added to big molecules like proteins and nucleic acids after they are made. The methyl group gets in the way of binding to some things and provides a docking site for other molecules to bind, so this tiny modification really changes how a macromolecule acts in the cell. Everyone worked on roles of methylation of the nucleic acids RNA and DNA, but each postdoc or grad student was studying quite a different aspect of the problem, from roles in mouse development and rat cancer to differences between bacterial species.

Ernest and I discussed possibilities for my project. I decided to look at cancer. My mom constantly told her friends, "My daughter is a cancer researcher," and I wanted to make her words come true. I decided to work on methylation of transfer RNA in rat liver cancer. The transfer RNA, or tRNA for short, is small, stable, and easy to isolate; it's an important part of the process of making proteins. The tRNA actually translates the genetic code from nucleic acid words into protein words.

I was a bit nervous about doing the proposed experiments because I had never worked with animals before. "The liver is easy, in fact it's the only tissue biochemists use because it's all they can find. It's the first thing you see when you dissect a rat," Ernest told me. "The tumor cells are no problem; we have them frozen away."

He went on to ask me, "Do you know the definition of an

animal according to biochemists?"

"No, I don't," I had to say.

"An extract precursor," he said, and roared with laughter. He meant that, as a biochemical researcher saw it, the animal only existed to be ground up so its molecules could be examined. I didn't think it was funny. I thought about him before he retired as professor at City College of New York, where all the brilliant but impoverished Jewish New Yorkers went, with their subtle shades of humor. He was first Jewish person I had ever heard give a belly laugh, but I thought his jokes would go down better if he let the audience provide the laugh tracks.

Everything about him was big and loud and he was not subtle at all. But he was a warm person who interacted well with the other scientists at University of Colorado Med School. For the most part, Ernest had good interactions with his laboratory people, too. It was noticeable that he had a higher concentration of women than the other labs in the department. Unlike Frank Young at Scripps Clinic, he hadn't gone out of his way to set up a diverse lab by selecting among those who applied. He just took all comers, and most were women in his case. He was quite supportive to one of the men, Opendra. On the other hand, he was very cold to his other male postdoctoral fellow, Stan, who complained that when it was time for him to leave, he expected to have to sell shoes because Ernest wouldn't recommend him. I don't really know what Stan was working on, but he did come to the end of his funding and leave while I was there, and as far as I know he didn't stay in science.

In Borek's group, I recreated the good kind of relationship with scientific colleagues that I had in Appalachian State; our group enjoyed discussing science. Most of us were women, and I thought it was fun it was to have women colleagues. Since they knew I was married, they didn't fear I might suddenly descend upon their boyfriends or husbands like a hawk.

During the Borek years, I rediscovered scientific meetings, but with a difference. I had loved the microbiology meetings during college, going along with Ann Lacy. During graduate school, I had continued to go and had enjoyed a group of friends from UCSD whom I had met while seeking a graduate school. They always went out to dinner together, and kindly included me although I wasn't really a part of their group.

From Denver, I went to the Federation Meetings (FASEB, the Federation of American Societies for Experimental Biology) with the Borek group. It may not have actually been 100,000 people, but it seemed that way to me. It was huge, and even if you knew people, they weren't likely to run into you in a meeting that big. There were sessions presented all up and down the Atlantic City beach in ten or twelve different hotels in addition to the convention center.

Borek himself socialized with his buddies and former colleagues; usually he invited us all to one "lab reunion" dinner so we could meet people whose papers we had read and we could all network. The individual scientists from Borek's group didn't go around together at the FASEB meeting either, so it was a lonely scene for most of them.

Luckily for me, Richard went to the FASEB meetings to search for great prices on new apparatus, working his contacts in the enormous exhibits by scientific supply companies. The salesmen invited us to parties. I felt a bit uncomfortable there, since both salesmen and scientists along for the events seemed to be hitting on an unending stream of young girls, probably naïve graduate students. There was lots of drinking and dancing, and no one talked science. I was out of the scientific loop. I tried to cheer myself up by buying new clothes for these fancy occasions.

Richard's friend Howie once told me he loved to go to meetings because he picked up so much scientific information there and had great discussions with his former colleagues. I felt sad, because I couldn't recall any such experience, after my time with Ann Lacy. Meetings weren't focused on science when I went with Richard, but were scary when I went by myself. Then, I often had no one to eat with. Sometimes I went to dinner with the one or two men who felt it was okay to go to dinner with me, only to see many tables filled with scientists throwing out precarious charm to female graduate students they were with. I missed that scientific stimulation and updating I needed from meetings. I depended on Borek's ability to collect the latest scoops that weren't yet published.

During my years with Borek, I became friends with two women who were very interested in feminism. Nancy and Carol took me along to feminist meetings, and told me about reading Betty Friedan's book, and more recently Shulamith Firestone's. They lent me the books, and as I read them, I talked with the two of them. We all looked at how the things we read might apply to our own lives. I got out a lot of the bad things I'd frozen away in the freezer in back of my mind and thought them over. Nancy and Carol were not working, thought over whether they wanted to work, or if they would still feel like valuable, important persons without working. They felt I was ahead of them, since I had a PhD and a job of sorts. I felt like they understood these issues so much better and faster than I had, I was behind them.

I thought in retrospect that laws were helpful (Carol was inclined then to think they were useless). I'd felt the sting of what men had said to me when I was seeking a graduate school, and I knew that laws had made the society behave better to women. Carol, and to a degree Nancy as well, thought that hearts weren't changed by laws, and that until hearts changed, no real progress could be made. I had a long talk with Richard about that idea, and he said he completely disagreed. He felt that if you could control people's behavior, and make bad behavior cost them enough, then things were much improved for the targets of discrimination.

"It just takes one black person in a board meeting to stop the jokes, to stop the anecdotes about putting blacks down. Works the same way for women, I guess. Tokens are kind of powerless in a way, but they do have the power to influence the atmosphere, and never doubt that helps." I think he was probably right. I imagined myself at a table with a group of marine ecologists, deciding if women could go on an oceanography cruise. It seemed clear that different kinds of things would be said with me present than if no woman were there.

I had given a number of talks during the four years I was in Borek's laboratory, and eventually it occurred to me that I was actually beginning to enjoy explaining things to an audience. Eureka, I could consider becoming a professor! But I had limited teaching experience. Teaching lab at Yale had been so personal and technique-oriented that it hadn't pushed my "speaking in public, oh no" buttons and I had really enjoyed it.

Now that I was beginning to enjoy giving science talks, I thought that I needed to be able to show some lecturing on my Curriculum Vitae. I asked Borek if he knew of any opportunities. He said a group of graduate students were organizing a course on microbial genetics and each planned to teach two weeks. I could teach two weeks on genetics of fungi if I wanted to do it. I was excited, and agreed right away. That class, for a mixture of advanced medical students interested in infectious diseases and graduate students, went very well. It really encouraged me to think more about being a professor instead of our-lady-of-perpetual-research. Walden Roberts, one of the best teachers at University of Colorado Medical School at the time, taught us to limit the big messages per lecture to three points, with supporting material for each one, and to recap at the end. Thinking about how to teach was almost as interesting as doing research.

I learned a lot from my postdoc with Ernest, about science and how science works. I presented my work at meetings for the first time, and Ernest mentored me in preparing so that I could answer questions about the work with authority. I learned that you need to answer questions about the background of your entire field. Hostile scientists who thought methylation was "simple rococo without function", or that tRNA was unimportant compared to messenger RNA, came to ask questions that they hoped would

embarrass Ernest. I needed to have good answers to these "attack questions" and we had prep sessions to get those answers ready. We didn't give posters in those days; short platform talks were the presentation style.

Once I talked at the FASEB meeting about how estrogen turns on egg white proteins, not only by inducing messenger RNA, but also by controlling methylation of the small helper transfer RNAs. My talk was scheduled in a tiny room at the top of the convention center in Atlantic City, NJ. When I saw the room, I was sure no one could find it and I was about to give my talk to the spiders in the corners. But the organizers had underestimated the response. The room filled to capacity and then there were people standing in the hall. My former biochemistry professor from Yale, was there, with his little notebook. He was famous for including updates from that black notebook in his biochemistry lectures. I was amazed and gratified to have such a large, interested audience. The "attack questions" didn't faze me, thanks to Borek's careful preparation.

Borek was also a good mentor about picking problems and deciding when to publish. He said, "We're looking for a phenomenon. Once we have that, there's lots of work we can do to define and explore it." A phenomenon, in his terms, was a new role or potential role for methylation in regulating some aspect of biology. In general, it was an observation that suggested new territory to explore scientifically.

In his lab, I started by exploring his wife Sylvia's phenomenon that in cancer cells, the little helper transfer RNAs had very few methyl groups. Her phenomenon was so productive that she couldn't explore all of its aspects by herself. Then, I went on find a new phenomenon: sex hormones that control female chicken development exert strong effects on methylation of transfer RNA, the project I later discussed at FASEB. Finally, I detected another new phenomenon, the methylation of transfer RNA decreased during aging of rats. I was interested in aging, and started reading a lot of papers on the subject. I decided that when I left the lab, I wanted to continue that study, and Ernest kindly agreed

I could take that along with me as my own project. His lab would no longer work on aging and methylation after I left, he told me.

"We can afford to let you take a phenomenon, because we have a lot more phenomena we're investigating now and even more ideas," he said. "You should always work with people who have a lot of ideas, because then they will never need to steal yours."

In addition to all the rest, Borek mentored me in writing my first grant proposal. "You need to read this article I wrote," he said, handing me a reprint. He argued in the reprinted article that scientists should ask for a grant for what they were almost finished studying! They would have a good case and get the grant funded. Then they could use the money for pilot studies to get the next grant. His paper had been published by a prestigious journal, in an effort to reform the way science funding was granted, so that newer and riskier science would be funded. But no changes had been made, and Borek told me that what he had written was still the best way to think about grants.

He was absolutely right that without nearly publishable data, it wasn't possible to get a grant. The funding agencies are always looking to fund "the million dollar sure thing" without realizing that if you already have the results, you must be doing something else with the money. And what else besides getting ready to apply for the subsequent grant? In a way it's a stupid system, because what they SHOULD want is to fund the next breakthrough. But some grants where scientists hope for a breakthrough don't pan out, and the money might seem to be wasted. Other high risk novel projects succeed spectacularly. Unfortunately, you can't tell in advance which ones will be the winners.

Borek also told me, "You must put in your proposal other people's results that aren't published yet, as personal communication. When you have it written, I will read it and make some suggestions for whom you can call or talk with at meetings."

"Why?"

"Because you submit the proposal in July, but it never gets into the hands of the reviewers until December. Quite a lot of papers will have come out in between and you will look ignorant if those findings aren't included. So you have to get them ahead of time."

For a long time, I thought he was for equal rights for women in science. In fact, when I said I was looking for a position in California because Richard and I wanted to move there, Ernest called up friends at UCLA and sold them on interviewing me for a faculty position, which was off the charts when it came to mentoring I had received about my career.

But then, when I was leaving the laboratory, he said, "Too bad, now I have to get Opendra another technician." I really didn't like that, because as a postdoctoral fellow with what I considered high level thinking skills and laboratory procedure skills, I didn't want to be mistaken for a bachelor's degree level technician working under another postdoctoral fellow. All in all, though, my life in Borek's World was a greatly beneficial boost in the world of science.

CHAPTER 11
LOOKING FOR A REAL JOB

The time had come. I had to look for an academic job. Richard had decided that hospital administration was not for him after all. He and his good friend Dr. Ron Carr had spent untold hours yarning and ragging each other, we had explored all of Denver's resources with our friends Sandy, Carol, Ron, and Nancy, and Richard had ordered lots of supplies and apparatus for the researchers at National Jewish Hospital at great discount prices, but it was basically a boring job.

He decided wanted to become what he called a "family lawyer." You probably have never heard of such a thing, and I hadn't either. He explained to me that families undergo divorce, not just man and wife. He wanted to learn mediation and the legal system and work for the good of the children involved. It seemed rather ironic to me, since he had left his three kids, Greg, Reggie, and Pam, with Margaret. They had come for visits, and Reggie had lived with us for a year in junior high school in Denver, but Richard wasn't a huge force in their lives.

Be that as it may, we decided that I needed to look for a real job (now I defined that as becoming a professor) in California. When I got a job, he planned to undertake law school wherever we ended up. We certainly couldn't live on my postdoctoral salary while Richard went to law school; in those days poverty was considered an essential element in scientific character building. Starting academic positions paid \$9,000 to \$12,000 a year in 1972 so we thought we could make it on that much.

I talked with Borek, and he called UCLA Biochemistry Department. I have to admit this contact was using the "old boy network." It worked; they said they wanted to interview me for a faculty position. I flew out to Los Angeles at their expense, and I gave a talk on my work on changes in tRNA methylation in aging rats. They listened politely, although I saw the department chair opening his mail in the back row during my talk. Then, I was passed around to visit briefly with each department member.

Ernest had told me, "For God's sake, show an interest in what they're doing. Don't browbeat them more with your own research in their offices. They're checking you out as a potential colleague."

I was not too sure how a potential colleague should behave, and showing an interest in their research sounded suspiciously like the standard advice to wallflower girls when I was in high school, to "show an interest in the BOY's hobby." But I needed a job, UCLA was a prestigious school, I loved biochemistry, and so I tried. But none of these men wanted to tell me what their own experiments were about. They told me about

UCLA politics, about their houses, their wives and kids, and they kept on telling me that I would enjoy talking with George (not his real name). Not one asked me about my own work and no one was willing to discuss his work with me. George was my last interview.

After the buildup, I thought he must be a golden analytic brain or a person of enormous charisma. No one had said why I must meet him, though.

George was black. He was working on the biochemistry of virus infections. He was very nervous and jumpy, but he was at least willing to tell me what he worked on.

At the time, I was at a loss to understand the buildup around this meeting. It finally hit me on the plane on the way back. We were both outcasts; he was a token minority person, and I was being interviewed as a potential token woman scientist. I never received a letter about their decision; dead silence eloquently summarized their interest in me as a candidate.

Borek asked me every day for a week if I had received a call, then called one of his friends. "Well, we didn't really have a position open," he was told.

He came down the hall to my office to tell me about the phone call. "I guess times have changed," he said, ruffling his black hair in frustration. "You'll have to read the ads and apply for positions now. It all used to be so much more civilized."

"If you were a man, maybe," I said.

"No, I'm sure their response had nothing to do with your gender," he told me.

I was just as sure he was wrong. I became best friends with *Science*, the journal that published virtually all of the position announcements. Every issue, I marked up the ads, tailored my application packet to what was wanted, and sent it in. Every one of those search chairs got a personal letter crafted in response to that particular advertisement. There had to have been a hundred or more. I applied to everything "West of Philadelphia," as Ernest once said peevishly. He was willing to write all of those letters of recommendation, but wasn't really convinced that this was the right way for the process to work. In those days, every single application required three letters of recommendation; there was none of this "names of references from whom we can solicit references if we wish to pursue your application." It was before the days of word processing computers, too. No wonder Ernest's secretary Lynne never really took to me after that experience.

The next bite on my fishing line was UC Riverside. They were looking for someone who had a background in fungi and wanted to work on plant immunity to fungal infections. I didn't know much about fungi that attack plants, but I certainly had some credentials in fungal genetics. That, with my tailored letter and materials, sufficed to get me an interview. At UC Riverside, some of my old friends from Scripps Clinic and Research Foundation, Bill and Nao, were in the department where I was being interviewed. Since I was interviewing for a fungal emphasis position, I presented my talk on my dissertation research. But, I shot myself in the foot by saying that I didn't want to move out of the areas I had worked in with Borek; I hoped to keep both the fungal work and the rat aging work going if I came there. I circulated around, and this time people were willing to talk with me about their research. Bill and Nao took me out to lunch at Love's BarBQ after my interviews and broke the news that people were very concerned about the animal work I planned to do; this was going to be the only position in fungal defenses and they didn't like the idea of diverting part of it. Sure enough, I didn't get the offer.

Next, Colorado State University, about an hour's drive north of Denver at Fort Collins, decided to interview me for a biochemistry position. I went up, gave a talk on my work with Borek, which they found interesting, and met each faculty member. I got along well with all of those men; they told me about their research and also asked me more about my own. They said they'd love to have me work on methylation in aging mice and rats. Richard, who was planning to go to law school, had found no law school in Fort Collins. He had to go to law school in Denver. We decided that if I got the offer, we would live in Denver and I could drive up to Fort Collins to work and back every day.

Colorado State prided itself on close student-faculty relationships, and also had a number of department events at night in Fort Collins. When I told them I wanted to live in Denver, their faces fell. They asked me to reconsider that idea, since they thought it would rule out making me an offer. But in my naivete, I thought that if they really were interested in hiring me, a little thing, private to me, like where I planned to live, wouldn't deter them. It did. They made an offer to someone else.

About this time, I discovered that I was pregnant. The timing was terrible; if I looked gravid, I thought sexist professors on the search committees might have all of their buttons pushed and reject me out of hand. The baby was due in February. Luckily, I had an obstetrician who liked his patients to severely limit their weight gains. It always amused me to visit his office, because he had posted a large poster of a pregnant man, saying that if that could happen, people would be more careful! Since he was so strict about eating, I wasn't "showing" and wouldn't for some time. Richard warned me that those bouts of craving for lemon meringue pie at midnight were sure to catch up with me sooner or later.

I was starting to get worried about finding a position, so Richard and I decided to attend the FASEB meetings in March so I could do a job search through their career office. A friend had obtained a job by this process earlier, and I thought it sounded awful but was willing to try anything by that point. I was concerned about taking a tiny baby along to the FASEB meeting. My Mom and Dad agreed that our child could stay in Charlotte, North Carolina with them for the five days of the meeting. That was heroic of them because they still had a bit of uneasiness around Richard. They hadn't yet met and fallen for our son Lyle, because he wasn't born yet.

The next two "hits" came at almost at the same time. University of Nevada, Reno and Occidental College called me for telephone interviews. Occidental followed up by inviting me to meet with the Dean of Faculty as he was passing through Denver on his travels in December.

"Richard, what if he hates the fact that I'm pregnant?"

"Never happen. I looked him up, he's a political scientist. They have some sense." Richard himself had been a political science major. But that was no guarantee for me. I was very worried.

It didn't help that there was a big snowstorm the night before the interview. The Dean had asked that I come by his motel near the airport. Our car was parked under our apartment building, so we didn't have to shovel it out that morning. The plows were out early, and despite my worries we got through with no real trouble. We only had to wait about five minutes to get out of our own block.

Richard said he'd go into the motel office and read the newspaper, and maybe cadge a cup of coffee. I walked up to the Dean's door and knocked. He came right away and let me in. He had a suite, and we sat down on his couch. He asked me to call him Bill, talked with me about my experience with liberal arts colleges, and seemed pleased that I had enjoyed Goucher, although I believe he had never heard of it. He asked me some questions about my different research projects, and asked if I hoped to continue research if I were hired at Occidental. I told him I definitely wanted to do that, and planned to involve undergraduate students in my research, as I had been involved at Goucher. He took notes, looked attentive and intelligent, and impressed me with his considerate manner.

He said never a word about my pregnancy, by that time very obvious, and seemed convinced I wanted the job even with a child about to arrive. It was an affirming experience. At the end of our meeting, I told him how much I had enjoyed meeting him, with complete sincerity. Of course, I would have said the same whether it was true or not, but I suspect most people can distinguish manners from real feelings pretty well. I collected Richard, who was watching a football game with the motel owner.

He asked as soon as we were in the car, "What do you think? Did it go well?" "Yes, I think it did," I said. Some years later, Bill told me that he thought women were at their best when pregnant (he and his wife had four children).

John Stephens, the chairman of the biology department at Occidental (or Oxy as everyone calls it) telephoned me to arrange a campus visit and interview. I had to set it up after the FASEB meeting. It seemed to me it was too much to ask my Mom and Dad to take care of Lyle longer. Richard said he would take vacation time from National Jewish Hospital during the Oxy interview.

When I got back to Denver, Lyle was born on February Ninth after almost 24 hours of labor, and I was thrilled to have him. I hadn't been the type to gravitate towards babies, and didn't really expect the depth of feelings I had towards him. He was a very hungry baby, and a very wet baby. I will never forget the day I learned the need for putting a diaper over your boy baby while you're collecting the wipes and powder. He peed in a perfect yard-high arc, all over the wall behind the changing table, and I just watched him with my mouth hanging open. What a skill! I enjoyed Lyle right away because he was interested in everything around him from the get-go.

Borek said I wasn't entitled to any sick leave to care for Lyle. I had to go back to work the week after he was born. I stuffed down my anger at Borek and during my week off, I walked around with Lyle to visit several local day care places. I found a lady I thought was very caring. The only thing I didn't like about her was that she smoked. Every day, I picked Lyle up, took him home, washed him off, and changed his smoky- smelling clothes.

It was very hard on Richard and me to leave Lyle with my Mom and Dad so we could go to FASEB. The FASEB job search process is called the "cattle call" by my friends. Industrial, academic, and international recruiters attend their Career Center in droves. Each candidate puts her Curriculum Vitae into their system. The potential employers read the resumes that fulfill some criterion they specify and select ones to interview. Candidates get a sheaf of interview slips each morning, and must report to the interview area for each appointment. The interviewer sits at a table the size of a grade school desk-top, with one chair on either side of it. There are hundreds of these desks with interviewers in a screened off area at the meeting. You have to show an interview slip to get in. Then you go to the table number on the slip and sit down. You get a ten minute interview. It's tempting to say, "Moo" as you sit down. It's hard to hear your interviewer, since virtually every desk has an interview in progress.

If it goes well, the interviewer will often invite you to a meal or arrange to meet you later. I was interviewed for innumerable molecular biochemistry positions in the pharmaceutical industry. University of Nevada, Reno had an interviewer there who talked with me. He told me they were interested but didn't need to follow up, since they already had information from my earlier application. He said they would be in touch after the meeting.

The most interesting interview I had was with a male recruiter from King Faisal University in Saudi Arabia. They wanted a woman biochemist to go to Riyadh and teach women medical students. They offered a huge salary plus travel perks, and when they heard about Lyle, they said he could go to school in India at their expense. But, I'd have to wear a complete body covering whenever I left home, and I couldn't drive a car. They told me that Richard could drive me out to get groceries, etc. What interested me was that this medical education was one of the few intellectual activities permitted to Saudi women. Since a male doctor couldn't touch or see a woman, it was necessary for the women to be trained as doctors. But the constraints were too much for me.

When I visited to Occidental College, right after the FASEB meeting, I felt as if I were coming home. The atmosphere was similar to Goucher College. Their openness to both people and learning, I really enjoyed. The incumbent molecular genetics professor, Ann, was still there, and I talked with her briefly. She told me that the college was beginning to put more emphasis on research and that she had been caught in the transition. She thought she was going to have one paper published by the time she left, but hadn't had it for the tenure decision and was denied. She said she had liked the department and the students, though. I liked them, too.

When I left, Department Chairman John Stephens told me that I could expect to hear in two weeks. Meanwhile, I thought that University of Nevada might call. I read about their department just in case. The two weeks passed with no word. Then the phone in my shared lab in Borek's suite rang.

I picked it up, and John Stephens said, "They're going to make you an offer." He proceeded to give me a few tips for negotiating startup funding and salary with the dean, congratulated me, and hung up. I sat down on my tall stool and just grinned.

"Got it?" asked Margaret, my lab mate, busily spooling DNA while she talked. "Yep, I got it!"

"Where?"

"Occidental College in Los Angeles."

"Isn't Los Angeles where your aging friend Tuck is located?"

"Yes, at University of Southern California. It'll be easier to collaborate when we're closer together." Little did I know, in LA, a lab across town might as well be across the country most of the time, especially at rush hour.

"Well, congratulations! Call me from Hollywood when you cast your next movie." she said. Funnily, neither of us thought that I should wait to hear about the other potential iron in the fire. I accepted Oxy, and almost immediately University of Nevada called to ask me for an interview. I told them I was no longer on the market. We were California bound!

CHAPTER 12
SETTLING IN AT OXY

Richard and I had moved to Los Angeles in 1973 with Lyle, driving to LA from Denver and stopping to see beautiful scenery in places like Zion National Park. We had a little pack to carry Lyle in, so we could even take hikes. Occidental offered us a rental house just off the campus, at slightly below market price, and we were pleased to accept it. Later we found out that certain of these small houses had auspicious histories. Mine had been rented by some of the most illustrious faculty members at Occidental. Others seemed cursed, where none of the junior faculty who rented them had ever received tenure.

I had worked at planning my first course, Molecular Biology and Genetics with laboratory, over the whole summer before I came, along with writing my National Institutes of Health (NIH) grant proposal with Borek's advice and consent. At Occidental, we were on the quarter system, with three quarters per academic year, each lasting about 10 weeks. In each one, I taught one course with its laboratory. That first class, Molecular Biology and Genetics for juniors and seniors, was packed for a small school; 70 students registered.

The laboratory preparation for my courses was up to me to organize. Almost as soon as I arrived, I sorted and placed equipment and supplies in the teaching lab and ordered new bacteria and small equipment for my upcoming courses. The stockroom manager, Georgene, came to talk with me one day while I worked.

"You can forget this job. They must not have known about your little black hubby when they hired you. Enjoy it fast, 'cause you'll never get tenure here." Not waiting for my response, she turned on her heel and returned to the stockroom. I felt uneasy about what she said, but I never felt any prejudice from my colleagues. She quit after my first year and as she packed to leave, she told me, 'You remember what I told you. Those smiling faces can cover a lot." Her threat was actually the only negative treatment that I encountered.

I had planned that my students would isolate their own mutants of the famous bacterium *E. coli*. Each student could "own" their particular mutant, which according to plan would be sensitive to cold temperatures but healthy at high temperatures. They would locate the gene that was changed in their own mutant on the genetic map, and look to see if their mutant could make important cellular components such as RNA and protein.

I hired two Teaching Assistants or TAs, Ann and Sue, to help me in the laboratory. Ann was tall and blonde, with a calmness that was a great asset to the frantic prep sessions for this class. Sue was brunette; she had an off-beat sense of humor that cheered us when we were working overtime. The TAs came in at night and on weekends to help me make all of the agar dishes of medium (bacterial food) that we needed. The experiments went very well, and Peter, Kenji, Paul, and another Paul all decided they wanted to do research with me based on that class experience. I was off to a great start, except that having no women among my student researchers worried me a little. But that corrected itself with time; Ann even did a masters degree with me after she was graduated from Occidental.

As soon as I arrived, Rose Wang came to talk with me about

becoming my graduate student. She had been an undergraduate at University of Wisconsin and done research at the famous Enzyme Institute there. I liked her a lot, and immediately agreed to be her graduate mentor. Oxy had a tiny masters' degree program in two or three fields including biology. The program was purely research-based. Most of the graduate students were ESL students, trying to improve language skills for graduate or medical school in the future, but a few were just thinking over what came next in their lives.

My second trimester course went well, but the third trimester was really unpleasant. Peter had convinced me to try a non-graded (self-graded) course format for Biochemistry, based on the model of a course being taught at CalTech by Leroy Hood and his collaborators. I knew Leroy's brother Myron, a math professor at Oxy. Myron told me Lee had said the self-grading worked very well. You set up the standards for what would deserve an A, and as long as the students got to those standards that's what they received. I already hated grading and thought it was the worst part of my job. A good friend among the students in my very first class had earned a C+ and when I gave her that grade, she never forgave me. I had to grade students with integrity, but I was happy that there might be a more low key and student-dependent way to do it.

I used Lehninger for my text for the biochemistry class and used a problem-based learning book produced by the same Caltech biochemists who had invented that self- grading system. At first the course was fine. But, as the 50 students realized that I wasn't really grading them, many of them stopped coming to class. Those who did come mostly talked among themselves throughout the class, sometimes so loudly that I couldn't keep to my own train of thought. I was drawing all of the molecules in the pathways on the board, and the noise really bothered me. I repeatedly asked them to remain quiet, but they wouldn't. In class I often felt that something that awful couldn't be really happening to me, it must be a bad dream.

After the course was over, I met with John Stephens, my department chair, and told him what had happened. When I explained the grading method to him, he cracked up, laughing so hard he made himself cough. He commented that although the Caltech student geniuses were certainly able to handle this method, I needed to keep the upper hand over the unruly and rambunctious Oxy students. I told him that I wouldn't be using this method of grading again, and that I was going to redesign the whole course. He laughed again, said he knew that I knew a lot of biochemistry and could make this a good course, and sent me on my way.

Later, Frank from Chemistry came down and told me one of his students had told him I was writing all of the compounds on the board. He showed me a great system of multi colored dittos that he used to make handouts for his P Chem classes, and recommended that I use handouts for the pathways. That was very good advice, and I did that for the next year. The review of my first year by the personnel committee raised questions about my poor evaluations in Biochemistry, but John Stephens backed me up and when the next year I produced much better student evaluations, the mess blew over without any harm to my career. My friend Edric in the languages program was not so lucky; one course in his first year went badly and his department didn't back him up; he fell into a downward spiral and ultimately left Oxy.

In the research arena, NIH and NSF both awarded me grants based on my simultaneous identical applications to both, which was allowed in those days. I wasn't sure which to choose, but ultimately picked NIH. There were no specific programs for professors producing undergraduate researchers then, such as NIH AREA or NSF RUI. These were the "real thing"; the NIH RO1 type of grants that are the same as the big labs get. I was thrilled to be off and running in the research area, studying how informational molecules go bad during aging.

In Los Angeles, Richard was in Glendale School of Law. When I went to scientific meetings without his shopping list alongside me, I suddenly had hardly anyone to talk with, and going to dinner was a real problem. I was very grateful to the few men who seemed comfortable enough to have dinner with me at a meeting, such as Tuck Finch and Arlen Richardson. Most men, possibly fearing the possible sexual implications of going out to dinner with someone female other than their wives, or possibly looking to implement such implications with someone younger and sexier, or just being more comfortable with male colleagues, weren't "free" if I asked about dinner.

No groups like the one I had known earlier at microbiology meetings were to be found; I kept on looking and hoping to find one, but never did. When my students and I presented our results at meetings, I had a hard time even finding anyone to sit down with me for a cup of coffee. Gerontologists, with whom I largely associated in those years, mostly didn't feel like talking science with a woman. The camaraderie of science had disappeared from my experience at meetings. When I thought of Howie's remarks earlier about his most enjoyable experiences talking science at meetings, I felt sad all over again at what I was missing. Who knew what scientific breakthroughs were circulating on the grapevine at those meetings? I certainly didn't.

But my students were good and I was producing a lot of data. Rose Wang completed her MA and I hired her as my technician via my NIH grant. She continued to produce a lot of good data, which we published. Ann, my TA from my first semester of teaching, decided to stay at Oxy and do her masters with me too. It was great fun having her and several undergraduate students in the tiny laboratory day and night. In the summers, and whenever no one was in there, we expanded into my genetics and biochemistry teaching laboratory space just to keep from knocking each other over.

I bought an Apple II computer with 64 KB of memory; how huge that seemed then! We used to load it from a cassette tape recorder. We also put data from our double- labeled reverse-phase columns separating transfer RNAs from young and old rats onto punched cards and analyzed them using the mainframe IBM computer. I had taken a couple of computer programming classes, but finally had to hire an undergraduate math student to write the programs we needed to analyze our data. I still have one set of those computer cards as a memento.

We were testing predictions of a potent major theory of aging which explained why so many things go wrong in old age. The theory, propounded by Leslie Orgel, was called the Error Catastrophe Theory. According to its lights, at the start of life all with time, some molecules are made wrong. When molecules that make new macromolecules, such as DNA polymerase and RNA polymerase, are made with errors, that increases the chance of more errors. The whole process stimulates itself in a positive feedback loop until finally in old age, almost no macromolecules are made correctly.

We were studying the transfer RNAs (tRNAs). These are the translators, the smart little adaptors that can read both RNA language and protein language. Surely if errors accumulated, we expected to see a negative effect on these tRNAs. We designed a lot of ways to see such errors, and methodically went about testing each method. Each finding was written up, presented at meetings, and published.

After three years, I reapplied to the NIH for a new RO1 grant to study this great system more, testing the Error Catastrophe Hypothesis, and got the second grant. One of my earlier undergraduate students, Juli Feigon, had gone to graduate school at Caltech. There, she heard from a professor that he liked to help professors at liberal arts colleges keep their research going, and had given me a good review on my NIH proposal. I only wish this sentiment had persisted at the funding agencies.

We were off and running with the second grant, and soon after it was funded, were invited to participate in an aging symposium at FASEB meeting, organized by my USC friend, Tuck Finch. My students and I were thrilled, and carefully prepared our presentation. At the talk, I heard that these presentations were automatically accepted for publication in *Federation Proceedings*, with minor editing. Ann, on whose masters degree thesis much of the talk was based, got a paper rapidly published. In retrospect, this time was my research pinnacle, a time of great students, high support from the NIH, relatively easy publication of results, and an exciting theory to test. I enjoyed it thoroughly.

Chapter 13
Losing Two Students

It is hard to explain how strongly college professors bond with their students, thinking of them in a way that resembles the parental. But, that is the main reason why teachers get up and go to work each morning. I don't understand death, I profoundly distrust it, and I was shocked when two of my students died early in my career. They died of different causes, and each had an effect on how I advised students that followed. I'd like to introduce these two students to you through my eyes as a young professor, partly as an exploration of how professors relate to students in general and partly as a tribute to their special natures.

When I first saw David, he had a shy look; a lock of dark brown hair fell across his forehead and I thought he was hiding his big, brown, concerned eyes and maybe his soul behind it. He came to my office and stood outside the door, quietly rearranging his feet from time to time.

I waited a few minutes to see if he was going to ask me something or come in, but finally I said, "Can I help you?"

He said, "I don't want to be a bother."

"You aren't."

"Well, you probably can't help me with what I want anyway," he said, looking over my right shoulder but finally arriving at the edge of the office.

"Let's see." I said. "Why don't you tell me what you want."

"Your Genetics course is really full," moving his feet back and forth in tiny adjustments again.

"Yes, did you want to add it? Do you need it for something?"

"Medical school," he said even more quietly than before, like a whispered prayer. "Your schools recommend genetics?"

"Yes." What economy of verbiage! I flashed back to a time at age four when I was coaxing my spooked cat, Smoky, to come down from a tree. What was David hiding from? Success? Asking for too much and thereby tempting fate to slap him down?

"OK, you may add," I said.

David looked shocked; his eyes opened wide and he looked directly at me for the first time.

"Wow," just a touch louder, but with no affect dynamics.

Joanna was different. She showed up outside my tiny office. I looked up and saw a decisive looking young woman, shapely but a little heavier than the average student, in well worn jeans and a T shirt, with a round, white face, a large flat nose, and a sheaf of out-of-control, extra wavy, platinum-blonde hair. She looked competent and her shining blue eyes radiated confidence. She told me she wanted to work with me on some research so she needed to make an appointment. I invited her in to discuss it right then, unless she was in a hurry. She agreed warily, throwing back her hair and twisting a strand between her fingers. She gave me the impression that she was a planner and not an improviser; having to switch from what she had expected threw her off. That insight into her character was to have a bitter resonance later on.

She said she'd like to start with a problem from the lab, but later she'd like to branch out to a problem she might choose. I told her that was exactly how I liked students to work. Then, I told her about experiments to test the "Error Catastrophe" hypothesis of aging, a model that suggested that more and more errors occur in making DNA, RNA and proteins during aging. My friend Tuck Finch at USC had just given me a collection of tissue from aging mouse brain regions, with matching samples from young mouse brains. I told Jo that I thought one or two students just starting in the lab could look at activity of a particular enzyme in these brain sections, to see if its activity changed during aging. If this enzyme protein had been made incorrectly in aging, we might see that loss of activity in our tests.

"You do have room for me then?" she asked, sounding completely sure that I did.

"Yes," I said.

"Can you give me some reading material about the hypothesis?" I loved that. It works well enough if a student picks a project and then reads about it, but the best ones usually want to survey the pool before they jump off the diving board. So I gave her a pile of papers from my files to read. She looked like she had just received a present.

Jo said, "Thanks! I will be back in a few days to talk more, but don't give away the brains meanwhile."

"I won't," I said. I tried hard to sit still and not to jump up and down with glee that such a promising student was interested.

David was taking Genetics hard; he struggled with the concepts but didn't like to ask for help. He believed he couldn't learn it correctly if he didn't figure it all out from scratch. In lab one day, I said, "David, will you come and talk with me about this set of problems?" I had written that on the bottom of his homework sheets, but he had not come.

"Oh, I really need to do it myself," he told me.

"Why?" I asked. "If you see how to do one problem, won't it help you to understand the others?"

"It's how I was brought up. Self reliant." He sounded much more confident about this belief than about anything else we had discussed. His back was straight and he looked me right in the eye. I told him that we were going to just discuss what is hard about the problem, he was going to do most of the talking, and we could see if that unlocked his problem solving ability. I said I wouldn't tell him how to work the problem at all. Very grudgingly, he agreed. He came. He worked out the answers himself, just from explaining to me why the problems are hard.

"Why does this work?" he marveled. "I don't get it."

I wondered too. I told him, "I don't know, but if it works, why knock it?"

He passed the course with a B. I had not "helped him" by showing him how to work a single problem. A student trying to solve a hard problem has never identified what is making the problem difficult. The answer to that question often takes him or her to the crux of the concept. Strangely enough, just telling students about this idea doesn't enable them to work the problems. It only works when they explain to me why the problem is hard.

Jo said, "Well, is anyone else interested in the brains?"

I had to tell her, "Yes, Gary is interested. You asked first, how do you feel about sharing the project?"

She said, "It's OK, I like Gary and he's a hard worker. Besides, he probably has more time than I do."

In the end, there was no difference in their analytical abilities, lab skills, ability to be careful in the tissue grinding and the assays using radioisotopes. But, there was a difference in how much time they could give to the project; Gary had produced more of the data showing a difference in tRNAs from the brains of older mice.

I had to say to Jo, "Jo, I know you were the first to speak up for this project, but I'm considering having Gary be first author when we submit it for publication because he has produced more data. How does that strike you?"

She said, "Dr. Mays, you're always fair...some would say

strict but fair…and I'm sure you're right, so it's just fine with me."

I was so pleased with her decision and also with her characterization. As a young woman faculty member, I didn't want to be a pushover; some of the male students had tried to get me to go out drinking with them and I had refused. I was trying to be more like a professor and less like a friend, although in the end I really wanted to be both. But, it was great to be told that students thought I was 'strict but fair.' I couldn't have expressed my target way-of-being better.

Next, she gave me an implied hard question. "Dr. Mays, we haven't really proven the theory," Jo said.

"You're right, of course, all we can say is our results are consistent with it. We need to find out if the molecules of transfer RNA are 'dumber' at getting bonded to the correct amino acid, if the methyl groups they still have are in the right places, if there are mistakes in the sequence of the transfer RNA itself. Many parts. But this is the first step, and we aren't expected to solve it all in one gulp!"

"But it's not really satisfying to publish a study that doesn't show whether the hypothesis is correct." I understood what she meant, but without publishing it, we might as well not have done it. I tried to explain the nature of the scientific mosaic to her. She said she was beginning to get it, why a publication is useful if you have novel findings even if they only contribute towards a final test of the hypothesis.

I told her, "Jo, you're beginning to develop scientific aesthetics. That is very important to you if you want to be a scientist; you can choose problems to work on that promise a critical test of an important idea or might lead to a big breakthrough."

She looked dubious, but said, "Thank you, Dr. Mays." She drifted off down the hall, twisting a lock of her hair and looking less decisive than before.

David's death was announced at a faculty meeting. He had been graduated as a biochemistry major. Not having been admitted to medical school on the first try, he had decided to work for a few years before reapplying. He had Emergency Medical Technician certification so he took a job driving an ambulance. Many of my students go into the medical field, and I always think about how I would feel if I looked up from an automobile accident and saw their faces. Some faces might terrify me; others would make me feel confident. David's brown eyed, concerned gaze would have felt good. His ambulance was wrecked when going on a call. He died instantly.

But it was not to be. David drove cautiously through a red light, but the car that hit the ambulance was going too fast to stop.

I was numb with shock. This was one of my kids. It couldn't be true. One of my students had died. I had never thought about that possibility, was not at all prepared. David had hardly begun his life in health services. I hated the idea that he was dead. Even today, with a lot more experience of people close to me dying, it's rarely possible for me to feel comfortable with death.

At that time, death was a stranger. My mother's father had died when Mom was only five, and my other grandparents had died over the five years preceding David's death, but my parents hadn't told me until the funerals were over. Death was a hidden, almost shameful act in my family, not something to be celebrated or experienced willingly. No Irish wakes, no Scottish dirges, just the long silence. I had a vague sense that I missed my grandparents although they had lived long lives and their times had come. I had not thought deeply about it.

One experience with death was more a threat to my dreams than call to think about mortality. While I was in my first year at Yale, a woman postdoctoral researcher in Giles' group committed suicide. She was doing productive research and helped with teaching Genetics. I liked her although I didn't know her well. She had symbolic value, though, for all of us women graduate students. She "had it all" because she had her PhD, was doing interesting research, and was married with children. We all saw her as evidence that we could pull off this difficult combination of marriage and science career. And then she committed suicide, becoming the worst possible role model, one who figuratively screamed that it couldn't be done. Did that mean we had to choose to be workaholic loners if we wanted to go on in science? It was a sobering message that I subconsciously rejected, although I reflected on it at times. Strangely, I didn't reflect on death itself after her suicide.

My first aching experience of death had been the suicide of Susan, a Goucher College friend. I read about her death the previous year in the college magazine. It was unsettling to me because I had admired her so much. She was highly intelligent. She was also very beautiful, with "good cheekbones" and long black hair. When we were in college, she found it easy to charm assistant professors from Johns Hopkins. Susan and Laulette and I had talked often during my first year at Goucher College, late into the night, about philosophy, utopias, and the failures of our social systems. I wished I had thought of Susan's ideas myself.

After I read that she had died, another Goucher friend told me she had committed suicide. I wondered what had caused her to kill herself. I had never seen her look enough to cause someone to end her life. You had to have given up on life's resources.

After I knew Susan's death was suicide, I recalled something else. Once in my sophomore year at Goucher, I had a very low period and I mentioned to my roommate Sherry that I had thought of suicide. Sherry must have told Susan, who showed up to talk with me the next day. I hadn't talked with her for over a year, but we reconnected immediately. Susan upset me profoundly. She seemed avid, feverishly interested, hopeful that I would tell her why I felt like suicide and how I was dealing with it. I was humiliated that Sherry had told anyone, unsure of the feelings and why I had them, but sure they weren't anything interesting or praiseworthy. I tried to change the subject, but Susan only wanted to talk about suicide. She told me that many famous women had committed suicide and she thought that society was terribly indifferent to what women needed out of life.

Susan wanted to know exactly what had triggered my thoughts of suicide. I didn't satisfy her desire to identify a societal pressure, having only the most inchoate ideas about why I had felt that way. Her interest scared me, though, and I never took that mental path again. She had somehow labeled that way of thinking as a road for thoughtful women who felt societal pressures, and I was more of a mental rhinoceros who would take her own road and barely notice whether society approved or not.

Now, I had to deal with the fact that David had died. As I said, there was and is a lot of the parent in me as a college teacher. I love to see mental and emotional growth in my students, and to hear about their later successes. I don't want any of them to fail, and will do whatever I can to rescue and support them. One of my favorite themes in counseling students is that it's never too late to decide to do something you love, and that you're willing to work towards. I have always been thankful that today, fresh starts and career switches are quite common. But not for David. David was the first one to have no more time. It seemed obscene to me, not just unfair, but beyond the place where life's patterns ought to be allowed to go. Screaming territory, a place of insanity and disaster. My wondering and chewing over Susan's situation didn't really help me to deal with David's.

Later, people asked me if I didn't think his parents might call me, and asked if I had thought about what I might have said to them. That never occurred to me at the time. I felt more parental myself. I felt a failure in my inability to protect a young life entrusted to me. Could I have done something that would have sent him to medical school instead of ambulance driving? Was I myself a good enough driver to avoid doing something similar to an ambulance? There was nothing at all rational about these thoughts, but somehow David's death had sent me whirling off center, no longer connected to my normal poles of relative comfort and security.

After I heard the announcement about David, I didn't actually scream, though a silent scream was ricocheting around inside. I walked around by myself all afternoon, quartering the campus, up Fiji Hill and down to the fountain, to Thorne Hall, back up Fiji, back past my own building. The second time I walked past the same buildings, I started walking very fast, maybe to release the negative energy or escape the fruitless and unrealistic speculations that I was experiencing about where David was, if he was still in existence, and why he had been lost to the process of living. The faculty meeting where I heard about David's death had been in the chapel basement, and at some point, I went back in the chapel on the ground floor and just sat, looking in pain at the abstract, beautifully colored stained glass windows. No one said anything to me, and I saw no one I knew.

Eventually I walked the two blocks to my home, and the sight of my lively, laughing son Lyle on his tricycle cheered me up. However, after he and Richard and I had supper and Lyle was in bed, I sat thinking a long time about Lyle and how I might feel if he died young. Meanwhile my husband Richard worked quietly on his law school homework with a background track of Aretha Franklin's R-E-S-P-E-C-T turned way down low.

I saw Jo shortly before her death. She had lost about thirty pounds and had a really sensational figure. She stood quietly ahead of my friend and me in line. She was buying a salad for lunch. Jo was wearing a white shirt with the tails tied high to show her slim waist. Her hair had been straightened and was tied back in a smooth pony tail. None of these fashion-conscious moves were like the Jo I knew, who worked in my lab in checked scruffy shirts and jeans, basic student slouch attire. I told her she looked wonderful.

"It's because of Billy," she explained. She was living with a boy and was evidently crazy about him. "I wanted to be worthy of him," she said.

Thoughts whirled through my head. Why didn't she feel her usual self was "worthy?" She was brainy, helpful to others, generous. I thought she had potential to be a great professor; she wasn't interested in medical school, but I had talked with her about PhD programs. I felt that perhaps it had been wrong to reinforce her emphasis on her appearance. I wondered about her plans for graduate school. I thought this might be her first serious boyfriend, and worried that these relationships are fragile. I hoped she would have a gentle let-down if they broke up; she seemed to have become invested so heavily in pleasing him. I felt an impulse to hug her and say I hoped all would go well and I cared about her. Those thoughts rushed by in a wink, but I didn't tell her any of them or actually give her a hug. I just smiled and walked on to join my faculty friend who had snagged a table for us.

Then, a few days later, Kaaren came down the hall from the Chemistry Stockroom to tell me, "Laura, have you heard that Jo is dead? They're saying she killed herself in the Greek Bowl because that Billy threw her over for another girl, and they think she stole cyanide from the labs to do it."

I wasn't numb this time, but angry with myself and guilty that I hadn't said anything to her. Hadn't told her anything about the high pain of breakups, but the long term survival-practice and worthwhile results of living through pain. Hadn't said that she was a role model for the classes behind her. Hadn't said how proud I was of what she had accomplished and how I expected more great things from her. Bad feelings to carry around with me.

Who knows what else contributed to or caused the decision Jo made to end her life? I no longer think that Billy's breakup with Jo was the only cause of her death. At the time, I felt that my failure to tell her my thoughts could have contributed. I still can't help thinking that a signal that I cared what happened to her might have helped.

Jo's life was almost all unfulfilled potential, and she was gone. I went back to Susan in my mind, feeling that a disorienting vortex of unhappiness that was hidden from others must have been part of each of their lives. I couldn't remember anything about my own feelings about suicide other than the scary need Susan had to hear the roots of the problem. Then suddenly, I did remember this: At that time, I was sure no one would care if I went ahead and committed suicide.

Why do people commit suicide? No one knows what's on the other side of that blank wall. How can this side be so bad that no matter what the other side offers, death is preferable? I felt like if we knew for sure it was nothingness, I could understand why people chose that road. The "perchance to dream" is still the catch to death, as far as I'm concerned.

A postscript to the loss of my first two academic children is that Gary and I finished the paper manuscript and submitted it; Jo's name was on it too. It was accepted and published. Jo was a coauthor on the very first publication I submitted from my own laboratory. Every time I look at that publication, it will always remind me to invest in the moment, not to put off anything that might help anyone. I can't always live up to this desire, but I try as hard as possible to "say it now."

CHAPTER 14
NIGHT OF DISASTER

Richard had gone to sleep a couple of hours earlier. I was grading examinations from my Biochemistry class. I added up the scores with a calculator at the teak desk in the living room. I noticed a note from Richard, saying that a test for the excellence of calculators was whether or not they could correctly complete a given multiplication that he had copied down. I smiled. He loved things like that, tests that could detect whether or not he had gotten a good deal on this calculator or a great deal, a steal. That day, Lyle had impressed me by standing at the window and doing a relative numbers calculation, all on his own. He said, "I'm four and Laurie is six. When I'm six, she will be eight. When I'm nine, she will be eleven." Laurie was our gorgeous and loving collie that we had adopted from a dog show kennel; she hadn't taken to being shown.

Lyle attended preschool at Pacific Oaks School in Pasadena. I applied for him to attend Polytechnic School for kindergarten. I thought Poly was a bit pretentious and stuck up, but Richard had convinced me to apply for him. They gave him a number of tests, including an IQ test, and had invited us to visit for an interview. He thought the interview was fun; they watched him playing with certain kids and certain toys and asked him questions about what he thought and felt.

That night, Lyle had been asleep for hours. I believe in a set bedtime for kids, and I think Lyle's was eight PM then. He fussed a little when his time came, but went to sleep quickly once he was actually in bed.

Richard was in his last year of Glendale School of Law, a non-accredited law school that boasted of reasonable success of its graduates in passing the California state bar examination. He struggled with his legal writing and worried about the bar exam. He spent a lot of time studying, and he also spent time sitting on the floor in front of the TV with a glass of scotch whisky, asking Lyle to recite the countries to match the flags in the almanac. Lyle had them down cold. Brown and white, jagged line connecting, Qatar. World on green, Brazil. And so forth. Richard enjoyed having Lyle show off this skill to visitors.

I traveled around the country speaking about research a lot, and felt guilty about leaving him and Lyle at home. I had not spent much time with Richard in the run up to this particular evening. He complained about a swollen foot the week before. I made him go to a doctor. Richard absolutely hated going to doctors. His usual procedure was to figure out what he thought might be wrong, chat up a doctor researcher he knew about it, then go to another doctor he knew and say he was taking drug x for his symptoms and could that doctor get him any samples?

I hated that, knowing that high cholesterol and high blood pressure were more serious than he thought and that he really needed to be watched by a physician. He had been rushed to the hospital from work once in Denver for his high blood pressure. Now in LA, he had even less contact with doctors, and was more at risk. The doctor he went to when I pressured him to do it was close by, but was not an impressive diagnostician apparently. He said put the foot up and it would go away. Or maybe Richard told me that, but never really went to any doctor.

Finally, I finished grading. I put on my nightgown and patted the ocean sheet on the way to my side of the king sized bed.

Richard knew I wasn't getting to the beach as much as I wanted to, and mounted a sheet with a huge and beautiful scene of breaking waves on a frame and put it up on my side of the bed so I could lie there and look at the ocean any time. I slipped between the covers and almost immediately slept.

I don't know how long it was before I was awakened with a feeling of distress. Richard was sleeping on his face. He made a smothered but awful choking noise.

"Honey, are you OK?" I asked inanely.

He continued to choke for a couple of seconds and then stopped. I rolled him over. "Richard! Richard wake up!"

He didn't stir. I tried to feel his pulse, but I have always been a very incompetent pulse feeler, and didn't think I could trust my negative results. I put my finger under his nose to see if he was breathing and didn't detect any breath. I hadn't had first aid at all recently; the CPR craze had come but I hadn't availed myself of it except in passing by watching a video. I tried to recall what to do. I checked to make sure his tongue was out of the way and began trying to breathe air into his mouth, alternating with chest compression. After about two or three minutes, I was convinced I was doing it wrong, and he surely wasn't responding at all. I had a weird sense that he was hanging like a balloon in the upper corner of the room laughing at my bad technique. I stopped and called the emergency rescue team, located only a few blocks from our house. The siren screamed forth, and in a few minutes they arrived. I showed them where Richard was and they started to work on him, using the defibrillator paddles for an electric shock to his heart.

I couldn't watch, and sat down at the big teak desk between the living room and the dining room, playing with the calculator. I tried that magic calculator task Richard had left on the slip of paper, but didn't get the right answer. I thought I was doing it wrong, and kept repeating it over and over. Finally, the EMT team came out and asked me for a sheet. They said I could expect the coroner's office workers to come to pick him up for an autopsy, that he was gone.

"But it was such a short time! Don't you usually try CPR longer than that?"

"It wasn't really such a short time. We have no signs to encourage us to continue. He probably had a massive heart attack," one said. He sounded kind, but his words were so painful to hear.

"But he doesn't have heart disease. He's only 43."

"I'm sorry, it happens suddenly sometimes," another one of the technicians said as they went out the door.

I sat at the desk, repeatedly working that multiplication on the calculator and getting the wrong answer. It was something to do; it seemed that I had to make the answer come out right. I must have tried it a few dozen times. Finally I stopped and just sat there staring into space. Lyle had slept through all of this activity, completely unaware that anything was happening. I felt very alone and suddenly felt like I needed support. I called up Dorothy and Dave Christ, friends whose girls had often babysat Lyle and who went to Eagle Rock Presbyterian Church, where Richard was an elder. They came right over. Dorothy made me a cup of tea, and Dave asked about the calculator and the little note. I told him about it. He looked at me strangely, but the two of them were very kind to me. We decided not to awaken Lyle.

In about an hour, a group of men came to pick up Richard's body. They asked me to sign some forms, and gave me information about whom to contact concerning arrangements for a pickup from the coroner's office later. Dorothy helped me pick out a nice suit and shirt that I could give the funeral home to dress him in for the burial. I put them in his small suitcase. That clothing made me start crying. I don't know what it was about clothes, but handling his clothes after he died just about killed me. Even a week later, when I had donated his clothing to others, I found some of his socks in the dryer and bawled.

Dave and Dorothy may have stayed all night, I'm not sure. A lot of that time is very murky in my memory. Our memories for pain are a lot shakier than those for joy, luckily for the survival of the species. The next day, I called Richard's kids in San Diego, his dad and brothers in Pittsburgh, and my parents in Charlotte. My parents came out to California first, then Richard's brother Clarence came, and finally his daughter Pam. Neither of his sons came. Reggie, who had lived with us for almost a year during his junior high school, talked with me briefly on the phone, saying he was very upset and sorry, and that he just couldn't come.

My colleagues from Oxy came over to help, and Jon very kindly offered to teach my biochemistry class in my absence. I really leaned on him for about a week, when I couldn't concentrate enough to write any lectures. I hated to face anyone, so seeing a class of students didn't seem possible at first. My research students sent me a message saying their work on aging was going on and that they were thinking about me. They said they were going to ask my biochemistry colleague if they had any problems. They signed the note with XXOO, an endearing touch. Our friend George said he wanted to write a tribute to Richard for the Oxy newspaper. I scurried around trying to find out when he went to University of Pittsburgh, etc, but George said it was going to be personal, not a curriculum vitae at all, so to forget that. George wrote a wonderful personal tribute, catching Richard's lively mind, great sense of humor, and kindliness.

An unexpected great loss can leave you with no vitality; it certainly affected me that way. Mostly I just sat. I wrote some notes thanking people for flowers. I went to visit cemeteries with an agent and my Mom and Dad. I hated the inexpensive ones, usually looking like if they forgot to water one day, the entire plant life there would join the denizens in death. Finally, I decided on Forest Lawn, Glendale. They had a double crypt that I bought, right on a lovely green lawn shaded by old, tall trees. None of LA was visible, and it reminded me of places we had stayed on camping trips. I think Richard would have hated the commercialization of that place, but loved the beauty of it. So his service was at Eagle Rock Presbyterian and he was buried at Forest Lawn. About a hundred people attended the funeral, many of whom he had worked with as an Elder of the Presbyterian Church. The only thing I really remember about the service, besides listening to "Ode to Joy" was shaking hands with an endless stream of people while trying to choke back the tears.

All this while, it seemed to me that Lyle was very matter-of-fact about losing Richard. Maybe he didn't understand it was permanent. But maybe he did and kept it to himself. I don't recall this, but my sister Jean came to stay with us for the funeral and she said while I rested, he buried his Wonder Woman in a shoe box, and then dug her up. She also remembers that he lay down in a little carpet-lined playhouse box that Richard and I had made for him. It had a tunnel you had to crawl through to get into the box. He told Jean that he wondered if you could get up again after you were buried.

After everyone had gone home, Lyle and I went to our respective schools each day and seemed to be functioning fine. I did notice that no one wanted me ever to be sad. People complimented me frequently on "how well I was doing." I had crying bouts sometimes at home in bed. Everyone thought I was "getting over it wonderfully well." But, I began to have strange symptoms. I lost checks instead of depositing them. I misplaced student tests. The last straw was when I found myself driving around in an unfamiliar neighborhood and had no idea where I was or how I had gotten there.

I talked with my friend Cecilia Fox and she said I needed a grief counselor. I asked if she could recommend any. She knew of a family counseling place in Pasadena that could work with Lyle and me together and also separately. I had never studied grief and had no idea that simply repressing my feelings was unhealthy. The counselor helped me to get my feelings about Richard's death out and deal with them, instead of freezing them into an icy core that made it impossible for me to function normally. With her help, I was able to get myself back together.

She said Lyle didn't seem to have any disturbing symptoms, but I should watch out for anything that might develop later on. We went forward, a family of two instead of three, missing Richard every day but trying to keep our chins up. Our favorite song in this phase was "Joy to the World" by Three Dog Night, and we sang "Jeremiah was a bullfrog. He was a good friend of mine…" loudly as we walked along the sidewalk going anywhere, making people stare, but cheering us up. I think we liked the idea of the three dog night: a night so cold you needed to sleep with three dogs to keep from freezing. We could have used a dog or two ourselves.

During that time, I was shocked to find that Pacific Oaks College had sent one of their college students to talk with Lyle about his father's demise without ever asking my permission or even telling me about it before or after. I found out by accident. It made me feel better about the fact that Lyle was going to move to Poly rather than stay at Pacific Oaks the following year, which I had been regretting. I hoped the student's interview about death hadn't disturbed him, and tried to ask him about it, but he just said it was a few questions, not very interesting. So I let it drop.

CHAPTER 15
WRITING *GENETICS: A MOLECULAR APPROACH*

Richard had died and Lyle and I were going on as best we could; the hole in our lives was not as painful as it had been, but it was still there. I knew that Lyle looked like a child of both black and white parents. It seemed to me that he needed to have contact with both white and black communities. I worried about his lack of black contacts, and wished I had the money to buy a house so we could move to a neighborhood that was more diverse than Eagle Rock.

During that same time, I became more and more frustrated by the genetic textbooks available, which had a lack of connection between genes and molecules. The authors wrote about passing of genes from parents to progeny, and in a completely separate section they wrote about all the insights based on DNA and how it is expressed to produce specific proteins. How were students supposed to connect the two when they were presented as "the old style genetics" and then "the new style genetics?" My students didn't make those connections; the examination questions asking how they were connected were often decorated with drawings or just question marks.

So, having a lot of time, a need for money, and an idea about what genetics textbooks needed, I put together a prospectus and sent it out to several publishers. I planned to begin the book with a chapter on the history of the concept of a gene, an idea I had heard about from Pat Wells at Oxy and had been mulling over and updating for future use. Then I wanted to connect fruit fly crosses with information about how the eye color or size was produced by the molecular biological processes. I wanted to use examples from mouse genetics, again connecting how the gene was passed on to progeny with how it worked to make the mice look or act differently.

Both Holt, Rinehart, and Winston and Macmillan became quite interested in the proposal. I talked with the acquisition editors at both places several times, and finally decided to go with Macmillan. I didn't like the fairly intrusive editing style of the Holt editor and I did like the large advance of $10,000 offered by Macmillan, which would enable me to put a down payment on a house.

After the contract was signed, I worked on the book every night after Lyle went to bed, when I would have been talking with Richard. It helped to distract me from constant grieving. I found a house in Altadena, at the corner of Lake Avenue and Athens Street, and made an offer on it. Lyle and I moved in, with a lot of help from the sons of Dave and Dorothy Christ, whom I had called the night Richard died. They moved all of our "stuff" over in a rented moving van.

Lyle's best friend Robbie and his second best friend, Shan had both moved out of the Eagle Rock neighborhood before we did, so he wasn't too sad to move to a new place. Through AYSO soccer, he soon met Chaka and Lance, who became friends and competitors for him until he went to college. Chaka's mom was white and his dad was black, and Lance's parents were both black. I was glad for Lyle to have friends who were black.

Altadena was very diverse; one of the neighbors explained to me that it had experienced white flight for a while when the black people started to move in, but then the real estate values became reasonable. White people, including graduate students and young professionals from US and abroad who didn't have a problem with a mixed neighborhood, bought up the empty properties and moved in. A lot of literary life centered around the lovely Japanese-style library about eight blocks down the hill from us. We really enjoyed the community, and went every year to the "Old Fashioned Days Parade" festivities. Zane Grey had lived in Altadena, and it had a distinct Western flavor, making Lyle happy. In Eagle Rock, he had once asked me, "Mom, why do we live West of the West?"

After a long semester of teaching and research with many nights of textbook writing, I needed a break. Summer had arrived, and my friend Joyce said she was going up to Idyllwild where there was an arts camp run by the University of Southern California. She planned to take ballet, and put her daughter Aya, who was Lyle's friend, into their children's program, Hummingbird Hollow. I decided to go too, and to sit at the picnic tables and write more of my textbook while Lyle went to play with new friends along with Aya.

Lyle and I were awed by the bright, clear individual stars and the Milky Way up there. I had forgotten how much sky was hidden from us by Los Angeles' smog and fog particles and albedo light from all sources. The dark, dry mountain sky was so full of stars it was stunningly beautiful. We cooked dinners with Joyce and Aya and ate at their tent, but I had chickened out of living in a tent and rented a cheap motel room near the camp. So, we slept in beds and I was well rested for all the writing I did there, amounting to two chapters of my textbook. From time to time, we went to concerts in the evening after dinner, or walked through the studios to see the pottery and paintings.

We returned to LA refreshed. All during this period between when Richard had died (when Lyle was four) and when he was eight, Lyle went almost everywhere with me. If I was invited out to a restaurant, a concert, or a movie, I took Lyle. He was a lively companion, and I also had little money so I didn't want to hire a sitter. He read or watched TV and acquired a wonderful stock of information about a new building project in LA or a political nightmare of some kind. Then, when we were out with my friends, he told stories. Many of my friends were convinced he was a genius, but he never thought so. He often concentrated on one creative aspect of an assignment and did the rest less carefully, so his grades were B's and maybe an A once in a while. He thought his intelligence was just average.

We didn't go out every night, of course; many nights Lyle did his homework while I wrote textbook chapters. I finished my book within a year of signing with Macmillan. Then came the reviewing. Macmillan sent each chapter to three reviewers, and I had to incorporate or respond to their comments and suggestions right away.

For the textbook, I looked for figures to illustrate the genetic crosses and molecular processes. I wanted to use a lot of pictures of how genes and chromosomes really look inside cells, but tracking them down was hard. Macmillan sent me permission forms for the ones I wanted. Macmillan paid up front, and then took the money out of my 10% royalties as the book sold. Due to my inexperience, I paid about $2,000 in figure royalties, instead of about $1,000 that I really needed to spend for the crucial photographs. I should have had all of the drawings redesigned and redrawn at Macmillan's expense, but I didn't know any better then.

The artists Macmillan hired seemed completely unfamiliar with science. They redrew something six times, each time fixing one feature I had complained about while ruining something else that had previously been correct. The last straw came when they actually traced my rough sketch after a couple of rounds of mistakes. I complained, and my editor was able to get a new artist that he said was more experienced with sciences. However, the first batch of figures I sent to the new artist came back with grasshoppers instead of fruit flies illustrating a classic cross. The illustrations were by far the most frustrating part about writing a text.

I submitted the textbook in "final form" just before I went on sabbatical leave to work with at the National Institute of Aging in Baltimore in August, 1980, taking Lyle. When we arrived in Baltimore, Lyle and I had to fight to keep him in second grade. They claimed his skills weren't those of a second grade student in Baltimore. I felt that it was a bad idea to keep him back because he was only going to be there one year. I could help him at home after school. I didn't want him to return to California and be a grade behind his friends. His first grade had been a first-second-third grade bilingual class, so it was no wonder he hadn't achieved high skills.

Once he settled down in school in Baltimore, he became a problem in his out of school hours. He would listen to me politely and then do precisely what he wanted, including leading his friend Nicky on dangerous romps in the woods all by themselves. He claimed he was grown, was the man of the house, and so I couldn't get him to cooperate with limits and rules. Finally, I had to get my Dad and Mom to come up to Baltimore for a week and help me get him back under control. I think my Dad's influence was what did the trick. Up against a real man, Lyle had to admit he wasn't there yet.

The hassle of book production continued through my sabbatical year, and reviewing the galley proofs ate some of the time I had been hoping to spend doing research at the National Aging Institute. Meanwhile, I met Mike Hoopes in December, and the book took time we might have been talking so we could get to know each other better. It also took time from hiking and skating with Lyle.

The book was published in 1981. I had a scare in 1980. Just as I was checking galley proofs, scientists discovered split genes in higher organisms. Let me explain. In bacteria, the gene is directly copied into messenger RNA and translated word-for-word into its protein. As we used to say, the gene and its protein are colinear; they contain the same list of information in the same order. Instead, higher organisms had split their genes into segments. The apparently meaningless interruptions between coding segments were "introns" while the segments with genetic code were "exons." Cells of higher organisms had to remove the meaningless interruptions in their pre-messenger RNA and put the exons of the message together in order to make each of their proteins. I was barely able to convince Macmillan to stop the presses by telling them that otherwise, we would be publishing generalizations that were lies. Genes and proteins were no longer colinear; a major idea of molecular genetics bit the dust. If I didn't correct it, our book would be out of date before it ever hit college bookstores. Two nights I gave Mike and Lyle supper to eat and retreated to my bedroom to finish the edits, but in the end I got the new story into the book.

My textbook sold well for about five years, finally going out of print about 1986. For a number of years, it was used by University of Colorado at Boulder; their order was often the biggest number of books ordered on the semi-annual printouts I got from Macmillan. I used the book myself, and heard that a good many friends teaching at small colleges did as well. There were also orders from Europe for which I got royalties. Lots of my friends thought I'd gotten rich on the book, but because I'd received such a big advance and had to pay off figure reprint rights, I never received any more actual payment beyond my advance.

Molecular genetics changes so fast that no text could last forever. Macmillan asked me to write a revision of it, but by that time I was married to Mike, already had a house, and didn't have a hole in my evenings that needed to be filled up, so I didn't. But I know that there are scientists out there whose genetics knowledge started out from my textbook, and that knowledge makes me happy.

CHAPTER 16
THE ESTABLISHMENT STRIKES BACK

Writing my text book spanned several years, so now I need to take you back and fill in some important details about changes in my life as a scientist. In 1979, I had been a Professor at Occidental for almost six years. My research was funded by prestigious "RO1" grants (RO1 means that they are major research grants to individuals, the most competitive type of research grants) from the National Institutes of Health (NIH). One day, I opened an exciting letter from the administration at my segment of NIH, the National Institute on Aging (NIA). They were planning a review of the status of research on biological aging. They invited me to submit a review paper on transfer RNA modification in aging animals. My own research, with a few other labs' work would be featured. They also invited me to attend a meeting in 1980 at Bethesda, the main campus of NIH. I jumped out of my chair and danced around my tiny office. I didn't take such an invitation for granted. I thought I'd made it in aging research. Even though I was a woman scientist, they invited me to be part of the major funding agency's "brag book" and symposium.

Part of the reason I was thrilled was because the field of gerontology isn't always woman-friendly. For example, a year earlier, I had been at a Gordon conference on aging where I heard sexist remarks from male scientists. Gordon conferences are very

131

small, about 150 people, all scientists in a specific field. They're held in the dormitories and classrooms of small New England boys' boarding schools during the off-season, but they're fairly prestigious. At this particular meeting, the only woman invited to give a platform-talk was from UCLA. Her talk relied on mathematics and physical chemistry and covered how certain proteins acted in aging rats compared to young rats.

The comments I heard were something like this. "It's a pleasure to see such a well built blonde still has enough brains to understand physical chemistry." This woman's brain power compared to the brain power of her critics was of the order of nuclear bomb to Roman candle. I strongly suspected that they had not understood one word of her talk. So, they focused on her appearance.

Somehow, I have never heard a woman in science say, "It's a pleasure to see such a well built man who still has enough brains to understand hormone secretion."

Back to the invitation I'd received. My students were excited about the opportunity for our work to be showcased in a book produced by the NIH. They met with me to discuss the best ways to convince people that we saw small age-related chemical changes like decreased methylation in the our transfer RNA molecules. Although they're small, the transfer RNAs are important; they're adapters made of Ribonucleic Acid. They help in the assembly of proteins. Their job is to bring the next subunit (amino acid) to put into a growing protein, following the genetic code.

We already felt that our results wouldn't support the main theory we were testing, that an "error catastrophe" happens at the end of life, causing ever-increasing mistakes in molecule assembly during aging. But we thought our results showed a slowing down like what we observed in aging people, so it was satisfying to be finding something similar at a molecular level.

I worried that I had no time available to spend drafting our chapter for the NIH's brag book on aging. At work at Occidental College, students asked me questions all day long. My son, Lyle, agreed to keep quiet in the evenings for a while so I could work it at home. Lyle had homework, but it was a pitifully small amount. I knew it was what he had been assigned because I asked him to show me the assignment sheets. I guess that the Pasadena Unified School District didn't believe that "time on task" was the best learning method for elementary school students. So, he watched TV once he was done, with the sound turned way down low. He was going to stay with a friend during my trip.

My students and I finished the manuscript and sent it to Bethesda for the NIA's conference book. Next, I got a letter telling me about logistics for the conference. We would stay in a hotel in Bethesda and be taken to the NIH campus in a bus. The meeting would be held in a conference room at Building 31, the place where panels met to review grant proposals and recommend funding or not. A list of the others invited was included, and I was happy to see my good acquaintance Arlan Richardson listed.

Arlan presented research at the same sessions of gerontology meetings that I did. His work was on the age-related decrease in protein synthesis in rats, and he was teaching and doing research mainly with undergraduate students, as I was. At first, we had circled each other warily, expecting attack, but as time went on, we became interested in each others' work and enjoyed chatting about both science and teaching.

Reading the materials I received, I was surprised to see that none of us funded by NIA and submitting manuscripts could present our own work. Instead, NIH had selected a team leader for each topic; he would give an overview of that topic. In addition, each topic had a discussant who was not a gerontologist, who would be asked to critique the work. The format struck me as slightly ominous. Maybe someone in NIH management, higher up than the aging institute, thought they had been funding the wrong grants. I wondered what outcome the NIA hoped for, validation or a new direction?

On conference day, I went to NIH from the hotel on the bus and sat down on the left side of a long, dark mahogany table. Knowing this room was where the fate of each of our grants was decided made me shiver. Each place at the table was equipped with a short microphone, so that our comments could be heard and perhaps recorded for posterity. As luck would have it, I sat almost directly across the huge table from Ira, the discussant for my topic, "protein synthesis in aging." He was a man of about 50, toothpick-thin and very erect. He seemed aloof and a bit pompous. He showed no interest in the conversation that a NIA administrator was directing into his right ear. He had a completely expressionless face, leaving me to focus on his prominent nose and thin lips. The lips looked like their natural expression was a sneer, although they were relaxed at that moment.

He wore a neat and sharply pressed suit, so neat it cast his credibility as a scientist into doubt. Scientists generally have little interest in looking "professional" and just want to be comfortable. I had never seen nor heard of this man before. When I got back home I looked up his work. He had spent his scientific career with the minutiae of ribosomes, the cell's factories for protein assembly. Ribosomes are important, but I thought that for a review of all of protein synthesis in aging, they should have chosen someone who had a broader knowledge of protein synthesis.

At the meeting table, I worried about Ira's background. I suppose the organizers wanted an outside eye. He had to lack knowledge about aging itself. Gerontologists agreed about certain aspects of aging research. For example, no one would report a response as aging if it occurred before animals were sexually mature, since the response might well be development rather than aging. And there was a consensus that aging was multidimensional, that there was no one cause of the process. He wasn't going to be aware of any of these ideas about aging. Tabula rasa.

The Director of the National Institute on Aging opened the meeting with a short statement. Afterwards, we launched into the first topic. I was not too tense at first, since my topic was scheduled to be taken up in mid afternoon. As the morning wore on, my stomach muscles tightened.

The chosen speakers introduced each topic in a monotone. They might as well have offered a disclaimer saying, "We didn't design or do these experiments, they were just the best ones we were offered by the gerontologists." Each discussant delivered his critique in attack mode, like the questions I'd been trained to respond to in Borek's laboratory. This time, I hadn't been given the answers in advance. From conversations I overheard I decided that NIH was on the warpath against the choices that NIA had made. Maybe they didn't like the Error Catastrophe Theory. What would our discussant ask? Could I respond convincingly? I became quite worried about my session.

The luncheon was served in the same room, and people chatted nervously about their papers, grants, and the meetings they planned to attend in the near future. Conferences coming up in Europe were a big conversational ploy as I recall. The staff took forever to serve the dessert and coffee. Finally, the food service items were swept away with a clatter and we were back in session. The afternoon topics continued in the same vein as in the morning. We had a coffee break right before my topic. I couldn't drink any coffee; the coffee odor upset my stomach. I felt shaky.

The presenter for our topic summarized the findings of several groups, including Arlan's and mine, in the usual monotone, staring at the table surface between sentences. He implied that our results were preliminary and perhaps our experiments were not done with the latest and most reliable techniques. He sat down. Ira didn't stand as some of the other discussants had. He leaned back in his chair, invading the space of the person to his left, crossing his knees without messing up his impeccably tailored and creased trousers, and folding the fingers of both hands together. His lips were compressed together so that they practically disappeared.

He stated, in his ultra-precise voice, that the topic of age-related changes in protein synthesis was potentially of interest. But, he thought it hadn't been explored competently. He tore up the concepts and methods of each of the research groups represented in the book. When he came to my part, he steepled his fingers, cleared his throat, and to me it seemed like he raised his voice a notch or two. I thought he felt he could attack me more strongly because I was a woman and the rest were men. He said something like this.

"Next, we come to transfer RNA modification. I have to ask, who cares if it changes? The transfer RNA still works, because the methods these 'gerontologists' have used to identify it require that it work, or they couldn't even detect it. I have rarely seen a study that was so little deserving of federal funding as the research in this area."

The way he said the word "gerontologists" was full of scorn. He thought we were all lacking in worth as scientists, and he had just said that my research grants should never have been funded. In his view I and my students were working on something that was so trivial that it was not worth studying. We had found small deficits that were quantitative rather than qualitative. No transfer RNA types had appeared or disappeared. The total amount of transfer RNA hadn't changed. He had implied that our methods would not have detected major quantities of bad transfer RNA molecules. He was wrong. If such bad molecules had been present, then the quantities of small RNA we had isolated would increase and the activity per unit would decrease, and we didn't find that to be true, so his criticism didn't hold water. It was a fact that our results didn't support the theory we were testing, but wasn't a slow quantitative change what the human aging process suggested that we should expect?

A ping pong ball seemed lodged in my throat. After Ira went on to lambaste each of his targets, he suggested that the aging institute should put out contracts (a much easier type of funding to receive, less competitive, often targeted to particular objectives and/or laboratories) in his own area of expertise, ribosomes, and lean on really good researchers to undertake studying them during aging. He was almost completely dismissive of the work in his section; he probably would have agreed with an iconoclastic researcher from University of California at Irvine, who later said, "The only good gerontologist is a dead gerontologist."

Our topic leader then stood up and asked who would like to respond to the discussant. There was dead silence for about ten seconds. Maybe no one could say anything, if they felt like I did. Finally, I raised my hand. I said a few words about the idea of slowing down processes in aging.

The discussant responded that no one was interested in details, what we should have been after was the mechanism of aging. Singular. Mechanism. Not one gerontologist in the room could support the idea that there was a single mechanism of aging in any known system. But did anyone else peep? Not after my effort got that kind of response. Was he trying to say that we didn't need any explanation, aging organisms were just going to fall apart? Maybe the second law of thermodynamics, which says that everything runs down in the end, was the theory he thought we needed. We certainly had spent substantial efforts on the Error Catastrophe Hypothesis of aging, a theory that could have explained the process but had little data supporting it. But he didn't propose that grand theory. He sat down, leaving us silent and unhappy.

In my mental record of the conference, the rest of the afternoon is blank. My mind tried to cope with the meaning of this event for my career. I kept going over and over what had been said, replaying that afternoon against euphoric moments in my laboratory and my students' excitement over their undergraduate research. What was going to happen to me? I loved scientific research and introducing students to its thrills and demands. Without federal funds, I couldn't do that.

My thoughts were jumbled and disorganized, jumping from topic to topic. If I couldn't get any more grants, would I become a drudge like some other science professors I knew? Repeating the same courses year after year from yellowed notes, spending the summers on the beach instead of finding out the secrets of DNA? Could I keep working around the edges, trying to break back into funded research on DNA in aging? Had I been funded only because I was a starting professor with novel ideas? A young hotshot? Now I was disposable and could be replaced by another hotshot, someone with even newer ideas?

Was this kind of thing why women fell out of the "science pipeline" that I'd heard so much about, the leaky pipeline that lost women and minorities on their way to becoming successful scientists? I felt small and vulnerable, a far cry from the confidence, validation, and excitement I'd felt when I was invited to this meeting. My claim to being a cutting edge scientist investigating important determinants of aging, possibly able to reveal basic secrets of nature, had been strafed. These inchoate thoughts rushed through my mind, almost faster than I could become aware of them.

I started processing the jolt that day, but it was going to take two years before I had completed the readjustment. By that time I'd have a completely different view of my place in science and what I meant to accomplish. I was about to begin the process of releasing my grip on the dream that I'd make a major breakthrough, win big science prizes, maybe even move to Harvard. I was going to come out of the two year re- evaluation knowing that I valued production of scientists at least as much as doing cutting edge research. But I still had to live through the rest of that day.

The bus did not come for us at the end of the session; we were to walk back to the hotel. Arlan and I walked together and morosely agreed to stop off for dinner along the way. What I did that evening was to grieve for my credibility at NIH. At the time, I felt like I was finished with the field of gerontology, that I would never get another grant, that I might never even have the nerve to ask for another one. Arlan was depressed to have been reamed out so thoroughly, but he didn't plan to move out of the field. He said, with perfect justification, that there were many interesting puzzles in the area that attracted him. He didn't see why one critical evaluation should drive him out. The fact that he went on to become a prominent gerontologist validated his reaction.

But I kept saying, "You don't think they will fund our future grant proposals with a review like that, do you?" He kept answering me that this was NOT a grant review, that we had no warning and thus couldn't respond as we might be able to in a proposal, that we could come up with new approaches, and that we shouldn't give up. He tried to convince me to hang in there.

Everything he said was right, but I felt like I had just been beaten up, and I didn't want to live with the bully on an ongoing basis. Our positive and negative reactions under the same gun interest me now, although I didn't think much about the differences back then.

I think our disparate reactions relate to a finding that Shirley Malcom from American Association for the Advancement of Science (AAAS) once presented, that women who get a C+ in Chemistry won't major in it but men who get the same grade will major if they like the field. I wasn't usually influenced by others' evaluation of my research, yet this powerful negative input overwhelmed me but not Arlan. I have considered whether Richard's death was related at all to my strong reaction, but I don't think so. I think that my reaction was rooted in my belief that the NIH had called my scientific ability into question after years of supporting me. It was an attack on my identity, since I was studying the role of DNA in aging and I loved DNA so deeply.

Their behavior seemed abnormal, and I questioned it in my own mind. First they funded me with hundreds of thousands of federal research dollars, then they claimed I was doing research with no merit. I was pretty sure the main health institutes were holding the reins, and that they had criticized how NIA had granted their funds earlier. But that meant I probably couldn't trust NIA; they would have to kowtow to the main NIH people whether they thought my research was worthy or not. I would have liked to avoid future contact with them. Unfortunately, the NIH and the National Science Foundation (NSF) are the only agencies that have a lot of money to grant in support of molecular biology research. NSF gets less money for biology by far, and tries not to fund health-relevant things that NIH should support, such as aging research. So even though I felt I had been bullied, NIH was the only game in town. The following semester when I applied for a new research grant, I had to swallow my pain and prepare it for submission to NIH.

CHAPTER 17
THE ERROR CATASTROPHE

The Error Catastrophe Theory of Leslie Orgel predicted an ever-increasing number of errors would be made in molecules as an organism aged. Each molecule had a small chance to be made wrong. Later, among the wrong molecules would be some in charge of making other molecules. At that point, the accumulation of errors would speed up. In the end of the life span, all newly made molecules would be error-ridden. As aesthetically appealing as it was, this theory simply couldn't explain our findings. But I felt an almost visceral connection to it. I loved DNA, I loved the logic of the molecular biology experiments arising from this theory. I didn't much enjoy "just looking" or "fishing trips" searching for a cause of aging. I didn't feel attracted to any of the other major theories at the time because they were indirect, focused on lipids or energy factories of the cell rather than its information pathways. Irrational as it may have been, I was convinced DNA had to be important in aging. I asked myself out loud when arousing from deep sleep one morning, "Should I trust intuition when Vitamin C was NOT fluorescent, remember that story of Albert Szent-Gyorgyi's about his intuition that it was, back at Woods Hole?" My morning musings didn't succeed in shaking my belief in the role of DNA in aging.

My students and I were running into a cul de sac. We should

have found a lower ability of old transfer RNA molecules to discriminate between different amino acids, but they were actually more accurate than the young molecules. Also, instead of having a lot of structural mistakes in their assembly as predicted by the Error Catastrophe Theory, the old tRNAs were well made, although sometimes they weren't completely methylated. A methyl group is a specific "lump" attached at a particular site in the molecule that helps the molecule interact with itself or other molecules. Methyl groups are attached after the molecule is made, and in aging, that methylation was less efficient. The old transfer RNAs loaded a little slower with their matching subunit for protein. An image of my grandmother slowly getting up from her chair came to mind. Slower, not riddled with errors, that's what we had found. It was time for me to write a renewal grant application to the National Institutes of Health (NIH), which had supported the research in my lab for two periods of three years each. I agonized over what I should do.

I had been unlucky (AKA wrong) in my problem selection within the area of aging. The Error Catastrophe Theory was a linear, logical idea but it had not been consistent with the data we had produced. We couldn't show that the molecules were full of mistakes; they weren't, to the best of our ability to detect errors.

Should we then move on to test a new hypothesis about aging? I finally decided that my best shot at getting another NIH grant was to bet again on the Error Catastrophe Theory and to continue testing its predictions, focusing on the burden of destroying or repairing the poorly made molecules. Then I'd spend more time during the next funding period getting familiar with the "next big thing" whatever that would turn out to be. Did I think that I should propose the "next big thing"? Why not? But I hadn't identified that idea yet.

I wrote the NIH grant proposal. For the first time, I was ashamed to ask my friend Tuck Finch, who had read each of my previous two successful proposals and made pre- submission suggestions, to read my NIH proposal. That should have been a clue, but I was oblivious. When you're ignoring all the storm flags and sailing out of port into the gale, you pay no attention to warnings. Instead, I asked my wonderful technician Julius to read the proposal. He really liked it, but the methods and ideas were those he and I had already been exploring so he wasn't a fair audience. It was like asking your partner- in-crime to critique a plan for robbing yet another bank using your usual method of operation. What I needed was thinking outside the box, as we say in 2007. Julius wasn't the man for criticism anyway, he was always upbeat and optimistic. He made a few suggestions which I adopted. I sent it to the NIH.

Six months later, I got the answer back. Remember how spoiled I was at that time. I had received a National Merit Scholarship to go to college, a National Science Foundation (NSF) Graduate Fellowship, and an NIH Postdoctoral Fellowship. As an incoming faculty member at Occidental, I had received both an NIH grant and an NSF research grant which I had to turn down because it overlapped with the NIH grant. My renewal of the NIH grant was also funded. I had always received every fellowship or grant for which I had applied. One hundred percent funding.

I opened the envelope and took out the letter and reviews. The first sentence told me about how many good proposals they had reviewed. The second sentence began "Unfortunately…." I sat at my desk and cried. It's easy to look back and say I should have seen it coming, should have expected it. Why didn't I know what would happen?

How could I think that submitting the Error Catastrophe testing again would work? I was almost willing myself to ignore all those danger signs that are so obvious when I rethink the situation. It was magical thinking, as Joan Didion described her actions after the death of her husband. I must have believed that if I acted like they would fund it again, then they would. If I expected the money, it would come. As I cried, one of my students stuck a head in the door, took a look, and left without saying anything. I wasn't crying out loud, but the tears just wouldn't stop. Julius was setting up an experiment in the laboratory behind my office, and he didn't know what was happening.

I decided to hide in the ladies' room across the hall. At that time, ladies' rooms had to have a bed in case a woman had cramps, so I lay down on that red plastic-covered, slimy couch, stared up at the ceiling, and scratched my nails slowly across the surface. Back and forth, over and over, in dirge-like rhythm. Goodbye to NIH funding. Goodbye to thinking I was a stable, productive scientist. Scientific career dead and soon to be buried.

I thought of all the students I had supported with summer internships, and how they had gone to graduate and medical school with my recommendation. I thought about Julius, and how his salary funding would run out in six months. More tears fell.

Then I started getting angry. I thought about how I had actually done what I promised with the previous funds, found out for the government that this Error Catastrope Theory wasn't strong. But, I cycled down again as I realized that I had reapplying to test the same theory. Back to the misery. I believed I had been doing strong science, certainly on a par with that done by all the other gerontologists I knew. So how had I gone so wrong? Maybe I should have taken time off to think up the next big theory, but how could I do that? When did I waste any time? I was working as hard as humanly possible. Obviously, claiming that Error Catastrophe wasn't dead yet wouldn't fly. Back then I wondered: could I have known that?

Eventually, it came back to me that I had been forewarned at that awful workshop at the National Institutes. The NIA (with a strong shove from the NIH administration overseeing them) wanted to take a new direction in its funding; they didn't feel like the experiments they had been funding were going anywhere. My premonitions were right, but so was Arlen. What I should have done was to define a new way to look at aging research. But instead, I had crawled back into my lab and licked my wounds, wondering if the "same old same old" would fly. Of course it wouldn't.

The aging institute would lose too much face if it funded the projects their discussants had vilified, just as I had felt the day Arlen and I had held our "wake" over dinner after the workshop there. I had that discussant to thank for this day, just as much as myself. I still had to accept blame, though.

If I had come to these insights a year earlier, I could have avoided this rejection. But thinking it through had brought me from a hopeless despair to a small flame of righteous anger. My research was just caught in a political game within the NIH. It was worthwhile, but I should have known better than to propose it in that way at that time. That was the real message of the awful conference, but I hadn't "computed" the right response. Now that I understood, I thought I might be able to work out some way of release from the mess I was in. But why couldn't they have just written me a letter saying, "The error catastrophe theory is no longer of interest to us, we must examine other possibilities?" That's not how the system operates. You send in a proposal, and they respond.

It had taken me about an hour to admit that I had hidden my head in the sand and to work my way out of the depths. I washed my face, went back to my office, and told Julius that the grant was rejected and that he could have time off when he needed it to look for another job.

He reacted with disbelief. He thought what we were doing was so interesting and valuable he couldn't comprehend why the government would stop our funding. My heart was warmed by his passion, but now I knew with some certainty that I should have foreseen this. Finally, Julius told me he would look for another position, or maybe he and his partner would start a winery and make meade, a wine starting from honey. He went back to the lab with dragging feet and a slumped posture.

I had failed him, failed my students, failed my son Lyle, failed myself. I had not listened to the NIH conference review, or more importantly, to my own premonitions. I was in purgatory, if not hell at that moment. It had been my job to see this coming, to avoid having this ton of bricks land on us. I was no longer a scientist, for what could I do in molecular biology without funding? Every single tiny tube, micropippetor tip, enzyme, and plasmid was expensive. It was all blown away by one mistake, and I was the one whose error had caused the catastrophe. I was thoroughly miserable, but not ready to give up. The tiny spark of anger was enough to keep me alive as a scientist.

CHAPTER 18
TRYING TO BOUNCE BACK

After the fall from the horse comes the attempt to get back up on his back if you're going to get anywhere. When I had stopped keening over the rejected National Institutes of Health (NIH) grant proposal on further testing the Error Catastrophe Theory, I considered what to do. I had received tenure and promotion. Occidental said I could apply for my sabbatical leave the following year. Maybe I could use that time to connect with a new problem.

In spite of the daunting conference at NIH and the rejected grant proposal, the idea of aging DNA still drew me. I didn't want to switch to cancer, which was "where the action was." I was going to break the mold and open the doors to a new paradigm of aging. I just wasn't quite ready to propose that new idea. I decided to try to go to the National Institute on Aging for its in-house research program.

At a small Gordon conference, I met a nucleic-acids-chemist from the National Institute on Aging (NIA). He seemed kindly as well as intelligent, and I thought he would be a good mentor. He agreed that I could work with him at NIA. The aging institute's campus is apart from the main Bethesda campus of NIH, in Baltimore. He recommended a grant program. I applied for this Intergovernmental Personnel Act grant, was funded, and breathed a sigh of relief to be back on track in the funding process.

Lyle was about to start second grade, and he thought going to Baltimore for a year would be a lark. He loved snow and he had heard from his grandparents in North Carolina that they sometimes had as much as a foot of it. Maryland might get even more, he thought. We were going to drive across the country in my tiny electric blue Dodge colt, so he thought he could see some cowboys on the way.

Just before I left for Baltimore, Don came by to visit. He had been one of the first graduates from the interdisciplinary Biochemistry major I had helped to found at Oxy. I told him what I was interested in and he said, "Well, you should certainly learn about this new technique called Southern blotting, but I'm not sure there are good tools for studying genomic instability during aging. I'd look at DNA methylation. Read this paper."

Don had a copy of a recent paper showing how to tell if DNA is methylated. I was interested because I remembered a lot about DNA methylation from my days in Borek's laboratory. The authors that unmethylated DNA was cut apart into fragments, but under similar conditions, DNA with methyl groups was not cut, making a clear distinction that could be seen using a Southern blot.

I was excited to hear about Southern blots. People had used base pairing with probes in solution to see if an unknown DNA contained certain sequences. But solution base pairing didn't tell them anything about the sizes of the DNA pieces that were paired with their probes. The essence of a Southern blot, Don explained, was to separate DNA pieces by size. The samples were loaded into slots in a jello-like gel, then the investigator used a mild electric current to make the DNA pieces move. Finally, after the pieces had separated by size using this electrophoresis process, the gel was "blotted" onto a piece of nitrocellulose paper. The DNA pieces attached to the blot were found by letting them form base pairs with radioactively labeled probes. Once the base pairs formed, the unpaired radioactive probe was washed away, and the blot was exposed to xray film. A dark line appeared wherever the test DNA had sequences that base paired with the probe. On the gel the investigator also loaded a lane of DNAs of known size, so the size of each piece that paired with the probe could be determined. This method seemed to Don and me to be a very important advance. We were correct, it revolutionized molecular biology.

The idea Don had proposed looked good. I quickly read papers showing that putting a methyl group onto the DNA of the control region in front of a gene could turn off its expression. That is, no messenger RNA could be produced from the methylated gene. I wondered if genes changed in expression in aging, possibly caused by changes in DNA methylation. I concentrated on DNA methylation as I prepared for my sabbatical.

At NIH, I wanted to study subtle differences in DNA methylation using a repeated sequence of DNA called the Intracisternal A-type Particle sequence or IAP. Mice had about a thousand copies of this IAP sequence in every cell. The IAP would work better than a single-copy gene because IAP's multiple copies gave a much stronger signal on a Southern blot than if I used a gene with only one copy. That meant that partial methylation could be easily detected.

Back in 1980, no one at the National Institute on Aging knew how to do Southern blots. The Southern blotting technique was new and it was a little tricky, so my supervisor thought I should learn it from an expert. He said he would find me one.

I worked on enzyme assays on aging rat liver while I waited to see how and when I could be trained to use Southern blotting. Everyone at NIA shared the tissues of any animals that were sacrificed. I used to go to my friend George's lab with my ice bucket, joining long lines of people waiting outside his door on sacrifice days. I picked up my liver and returned upstairs to study the enzymes.

Working with George was a young man with a sweet smile

and rainbow suspenders named Mike Hoopes. He was tremendously helpful to me. While I picked up my tissue, we chatted about plays or concerts we had been to during our off hours. One day I made chocolate chip cookies for all of the people at NIA who had helped me one way or another, and Mike took it as a challenge. Famous for his baking, he made me a batch of absolutely scrumptious chocolate chip cookies. Before too long, we began seeing each other.

About a month passed in Baltimore before my supervisor found a way to get me trained in Southern blotting. He arranged for me to go Bethesda, MD to the main campus of NIH, at the National Cancer Institute. I could learn Southern blotting in his friend Maxine's group. Maxine had me work in Francine's laboratory for my three months of training. Francine, much to my surprise, turned out to be a graduate of Occidental College. She gave me a small problem on repeated sequences of chickens to work on and helped me with various methods I needed to learn.

The only fly in the ointment was that Lyle's after school day care ended at 5:00 and the drive from Bethesda to north Baltimore took about an hour and a half in late afternoon rush hour. If I wasn't there to pick him up two days in a row, he might be thrown out of the day care program. Then he'd have to be picked up every day at 2:30 PM. I must say the day care in Baltimore at that time wasn't at all friendly to working mothers compared to California. But, Francine didn't mind my setting everything up and running the gels at very low voltage overnight starting at 3:25 PM, so I could dash up the highway to Baltimore in time to get Lyle.

Meanwhile, my relationship with Mike progressed. We had science in common, and enjoyed watching "Nature" and "Nova" on TV and discussing the programs. In later years, sometimes we sat quietly with each other, but when Mike and I first met, we couldn't stop talking, either in person or on the phone. I remember once we had talked on the phone for hours and I lay on my bed while we talked, so I accidentally fell asleep. I woke up later and Mike was gone from the phone. He must have figured out that I was out cold.

We discussed so many interests, finding places where our affinities were the same. We shared an interest in Celtic culture. Mike had tried to learn to play the bagpipe and had a chanter to practice on. I visited Scotland during graduate school, trying to connect to the supposed Livingston Scottish roots, and loved Scottish music and country dancing. He had never heard Welsh singing, and I told him about how much I had enjoyed it while touring in Wales.

We liked the same kinds of popular music, including songs of Judy Collins, Creedence Clearwater Revival, Eric Burden, Crosby Stills and Nash, Simon and Garfunkel, and John Denver. We liked to sing together, and Mike knew all the words to obscure folk songs that I loved. We talked about our families. Mike and I both were the oldest child and had to "set a good example".

We also shared a love of reading. I had been standoffish towards Michener novels before, partly because they were so humongous. Mike convinced me to read Chesapeake, the Michener novel about Maryland's Eastern shore, Mike's home country. Some strong Quaker women featured in that novel, and the whole tapestry of it was fascinating. It started me on a Michener kick that lasted several years.

Mike's father was a Quaker, and we spent a lot of time reading early texts from English Quakers as well as early American ones. I enjoyed the silent services. I experienced the silence along with Mike's relatives at an open-air service (they called it a meeting) in a grove near Little Falls, MD. A meeting house had once been on that site, which later was turned into a park. But they commemorated the meeting house with an annual open-air meeting followed by a picnic lunch. Mike would often go to the meeting in Baltimore while I attended a nearby Episcopal church. These two religious traditions couldn't have been more different, Quakerism emphasizing direct religious experience

while Episcopalians emphasized ritual. But we agreed both had strong spiritual emphasis. He did tend to say, back then, that my tradition had too much "mumbo, jumbo" for him.

Once Mike and I were engaged, he told Lyle that he would work hard to be a good father to him. Lyle wanted to connect fatherly love with the way Richard had treated him when he was four years old. Now he was eight, verging on a "king of the universe" attitude, and Mike was an introvert rather than an extravert as Richard had been, so it took a lot of work for them to get comfortable with each other. Mike tried hard during the run up to our wedding by doing activities with Lyle, like taking him to a pro hockey match. I've never seen Mike watch even one hockey match on TV, so it must have been a sacrifice.

Mike had insights into boys' bad behavior that went way beyond mine. One day, we were reading and had let Lyle walk up to the pool in our apartment complex to swim. I gave him a dollar to buy a drink, and expected fifty cents change. He came back and said he had lost it on the way home. Mike took him back out and found it buried next to the flag pole. I couldn't understand how he had known to do that. He said, "I was a boy not too long ago." Lyle wasn't pleased then, but later on he told Mike that his enforcement activities as a father had meant a lot to him growing up.

After all of my training at the National Cancer Institute, by Christmas I was proficient enough in all the techniques so that I was ready to take on the project I had planned to do. My NIA supervisor allowed me to set up Southern blotting in his lab. Before I arrived, the whole lab had been devoted to Nuclear Magnetic Resonance or NMR. The same technique is used medically to detect molecules in living beings, but for medical purposes, it was renamed magnetic resonance imaging (MRI) since people fear anything with "nuclear" in its name. I bought the equipment and supplies, pilot tested the method, and was all ready to begin the real experiment when I hit the next snag.

I was working at the NIA intramural research program at the Gerontology Research Center (GRC), where there were colonies of aging animals, and those who took care of them were understandably concerned about virus outbreaks. The DNAs I wanted to study, called Intracisternal A Particle (IAP) sequences, were probably derived a long time ago from a defective virus. They even encoded virus-like particles. But every one of them was defective; no viruses were released from cells. Even if you purified the particles from homogenized cells, they couldn't infect any new cells. I told the committee all of these facts, thinking that they would be convinced that the IAP was safe to study.

After deliberating, the NIA animal care committee refused to let me work on IAP there because it was virus related. I carefully explained to them that it was already present in one thousand copies in every cell of every mouse in their colonies. No dice. I was not to work on a virus related entity in the GRC building. Impasse.

My mentor's friends rescued me again. This time, it was a woman professor at Johns Hopkins who agreed to let me camp out in her laboratory for the duration of that experiment. She is a brilliant Chinese woman who, earlier in her career had shown that the histones, important proteins that are tightly associated with DNA of higher organisms, are present in a set ratio to each other. She found that each of the five major histones had different properties. Her work made it possible to understand the packaging of genes into the DNA-protein complex now called the nucleosome in higher organisms.

She even had people in her laboratory who had already obtained cloned IAP probes that I could use. Johns Hopkins was closer to Lyle's school than the National Cancer Institute, so I could work full days on the project there. I did the experiments and

I found evidence to support a substantial age-related decrease in DNA methylation in IAP sequences of mice. As Borek would have said, I had a phenomenon. I started writing up the manuscript on those findings, including my Johns Hopkins mentor and one of her postdocs who had lent me the IAP probes as authors.

Mike Hoopes and I got married in March of that year. I looked for an academic position nearby without success. When I asked my National Cancer Institute mentor Francine if she would recommend me, she said, "Why would I do that? I don't want to set you up as a competitor to me."

As an academic, I had spent hours recommending students and colleagues for many honors and positions. It had never occurred to me that someone who knew my qualifications would refuse to write me a letter; it just wasn't done in academia. But, Francine had the highly competitive mentality of molecular biology. I was able to get recommendations from my NIH mentor and Norman Giles. I applied for several positions, but got no interviews. When I went back to California the following fall, Mike went too, giving up his civil service position at NIH…the reverse of the other two body problem I had experienced. This time the man had given up his promising position for me.

My interest in age-related decreases in DNA methylation continued for more than ten years. During that time, I had a lot of trouble getting funding from the national agencies like NIH, and a lot of trouble publishing the work that my students and I had done. By a lot of trouble, I mean my batting average was around 0.333. While that's not bad if you're talking baseball, it's a lot of work per dollar if you're talking science grant proposals. And I had been used to 100% success, so I hated every one of these rejections. I wrote these proposals, updated the literature, included my new experimental results, at the same time I was teaching full time and supervising undergraduate researchers. It was a burden, and it seemed especially heavy to have to keep applying during the years when I received no encouragement and no awards from the government. After the fourth rejected proposal, I couldn't convince myself it was worth applying.

The comments of government grant and paper reviewers often said that no good work could be accomplished in molecular biology in a liberal arts college. The assumption seemed to be that bigger was necessarily better, that a small but well equipped laboratory with smart and skilled students had no chance to find out anything interesting. I had not received that comment earlier; apparently, it was thought that a recently trained person would be able to access help from a research university, but once someone was tenured, that grace period was over.

During that time I heard a radio interview from Hamilton Smith, one of the discoverers of restriction enzymes, a major tool in molecular biology. He said that the day of the individual researcher was done. No more "garage science" could be worthwhile, he said. Huge groups, well funded to do high-throughput research were the only way science could be accomplished. The NIH and NSF reviewers must believe the same thing. It gave me hope a few years later to hear Tom Cech, one of the Nobel laureates for catalytic RNA, describe his lab as a small and cohesive unit, more like garage science than factory science. But the funding agencies granted the credibility to the giant factories, not to us.

I am grateful that much of that time I was funded by smaller private foundations called Research Corporation and American Foundation for Aging Research. These grants were very welcome and rescued my career in science, but they were so small that I couldn't afford a technician. When I was in class or lab, my students could get into trouble with no one to help them.

The Error Catastrophe had been a catastrophe for me, but I had recovered, at least to a degree. I was frustrated because my funding and publication had become so difficult. I had lost credibility as a scientist as a result of being at a liberal arts college. Of course, I was a liberal arts college professor partly because I encountered less bias against women in applying there than at research universities.

But, I had tenure, my research was interesting, and it was continuing. I hadn't turned into the kind of idle professor I'd visualized back at the conference at the aging institute in 1980. I was able to keep mentoring students as they undertook research. The mentoring became more and more rewarding and important to me, even as I accepted the reality that I was never going to be a Harvard professor or win the Nobel prize. The wonderful students and their "light bulb" understandings of science rewarded me. Also, seeing so many of them continue in science after graduating from Occidental College was a thrill. Our group's publications and the small grants I received from foundations also validated our ideas as worthy contributions to research on aging.

CHAPTER 19
CUR RAISES QUESTIONS

Mike and I got married and he and Lyle worked at their relationship. We moved back to Altadena, California and shoehorned ourselves into the little house I had bought with the advance from my text book. The relationship between Mike and Lyle was difficult since Lyle was born talking and Mike loved silence, but they tried to get along. I worried about their relationship at some level all through the next ten years until Lyle went to college. Warfare erupted a few times, but they were mostly civil, although the loving relationship I was hoping for was fragile and often disrupted by arguments and bouts of silent treatment. Mike and I decided to have a child after we had been married for three years, and I got pregnant.

When the President of Occidental asked me to go along to a meeting at Carleton College about financing science research at liberal arts colleges, I was about two and a half months pregnant. Science funding was a sore subject with me, because a lot of the criticisms I got on my rejected government grant proposals were of the "that experiment can't be done there by this person, but otherwise it's a good idea" variety. I thought something needed to be done to increase the credibility of researchers in colleges. Maybe those at this conference would have some ideas.

Indeed they did. The President of Carleton along with his

Academic Vice President, Peter Stanley, had researched the problem and a good idea. We could participation in the Council on Undergraduate Research (CUR), a group of 12 chemists who had been organized by Brian Andreen of Research Corporation. CUR held that chemistry research in liberal arts colleges was good, publishable research, that such chemists also produced a disproportionately large share of future scientists, and therefore that funding agencies ought to support chemistry research in liberal arts colleges. Peter Stanley suggested that this brief be broadened to cover all sciences, and that CUR take on collecting and publicizing data on the success liberal arts college scientists. I was very taken with this idea, and the Occidental President and I agreed that we would willingly support the draft report.

At that conference, there was a celebratory dinner at the president's house, and unfortunately I started bleeding copiously there. I packed up with toilet paper and asked the President to get me to a hospital, where I spent the night. The doctors told me that I might have a miscarriage. Only time would tell. I was scared, knowing that I was 40 and nearing the end of my fertility; I thought a lot about how Mike looked holding my friend Liz's baby and how he had been married and divorced before but never had a child. About two AM the bleeding stopped and didn't recur.

At nine AM, the doctor told me I could be discharged, and said it was okay to fly. The President had kindly upgraded to first class, so I had lots of room, white starchy napkins, sweet and salty-smelling lobster Newburg, and water with ice cubes in a glass made of glass. I was worried about baby Heather, but I must admit I enjoyed the luxury. Luckily, she took no harm from this scary incident.

The next year, four biologists who wanted to form the biology council of CUR were invited to the chemists' CUR meeting. Mary Allen from Wellesley in Massachusetts, Bill Steinhart from Bowdoin College in Maine, Peter Russell from Reed College in

Oregon, and I were invited. We had been hand-picked by the Research Corporation people. Hal Ramsay, the Research Corporation program officer for Oxy, had recommended me, saying "Don't worry, she's no natural historian. She does real chemistry, even though she's a biologist."

All of us except me were able to go. I no longer recall why I couldn't. Mary called to fill me in on meeting. She thought we should become a council. She said that the chemists had their own agenda, which didn't surprise me. Working with chemist Jack McAnally to start a major in Biochemistry at Oxy had taught me about the way chemists approach policy. They collect masses of data on how things are going, for faculty and for students, discuss all aspects of the before and after scenarios at great length, and then after they make a change, they continue to collect data so that they can assess the effects of the change. Biologists, on the other hand, typically talk about a proposed new policy for a half an hour and decide to go ahead, collecting no data either before or after the change. In 2007, the culture among biologists seems to be changing towards the method the chemists had back then, but at that time, the two styles were very different.

The following year, we four biologists were invited to the CUR meeting at Colgate University in New York, along with a group of physicists who were also getting organized. It was wonderful to talk with the other biologists at the meeting, as well as the chemists and physicists, and to find out how much we had in common. We all gloried in the achievements of our students. We all thought of ourselves as scientists first. We all felt angry and disappointed at the lack of respect we received from the federal funding agencies, and at times, from the publications to which we submitted our research.

At that meeting, I met Brian Andreen from Research Corporation, the prime mover behind CUR, and his friend Scott Pyron, also from Research Corporation. Scott agreed to support the biology council, if we were approved. Once the biology council was proposed, the chemists debated it a long time. The biologists began to get dismayed. Had we wasted our time? The main argument against us was that we weren't ready; there

were only four of us and we had only the most general ideas of what we could do. But at a critical moment, Tom Goodwin from Hendrix College took the podium and gave an impassioned speech, not forgetting his inimitable deadpan humor, advocating both biology and physics, and saying it would require vision but that starting these new councils was forward-looking and would increase the influence of CUR. He also said that the biologists and physicists had unique styles, and he was enjoying getting to know us. I have no idea what he meant. We were overwhelmingly approved.

We organized ourselves as a Biology Council after being approved as a council of CUR, with Peter Russell as president, me as vice president, Mary as secretary, and Bill as treasurer. Being iconoclastic biologists, we insisted on being called CRAB (Collegiate Research Association of Biologists.) In long talks with the other Biology Councilors and Scott Pyron, we agreed that lack of respect from funding agencies was our biggest problem.

We also agreed that we needed to publish a directory of accomplishments, as the chemists had done, showing the many grants and published papers with undergraduates that liberal arts college and other predominantly undergraduate college/university biologists had produced. I became the editor of that Directory, and Brian Andreen published it through the Research Corporation resources. There was a very nice crab drawing produced by Brian's daughter on the cover, denoting the CRAB-name we had chosen. My husband Mike and I wrote an article for the CUR Newsletter, highlighting a lot of the strong achievements of the faculty and schools in the biology directory.

Back at the Colgate CUR conference, after dinner one night,

we stood on a smooth, grassy slope smelling the new-mown grass and admiring the huge old trees. Scott asked the four of us newly minted biology councilors, "Are you ready to take a national leadership role?" Not long before that meeting, a CUR chemist from Carleton, had met with the National Science Foundation administration to propose a new kind of grant, called a Research in Undergraduate Institutions grant. This grant had been implemented, recognizing that we had a unique role in science, producing the 'seed corn' young scientists in addition to good scientific findings. Scott wanted to know if we were ready to take on such advocacy. Our answer was no. What we wanted was to produce our directory and, wave it at every opportunity saying, "Yes we can do good science here!" Then we wanted to go back to the classroom and laboratory.

That was the wrong answer, and as we went forward, we learned that we had taken an irreversible step into a new sphere of science activism. Scott saw it coming, but we didn't. We ended up helping to advocate for the Academic Research Enhancement Award grants at NIH. We also revolutionized CUR itself. I headed up the CUR strategic planning when Stuart Crampton was president of CUR.

A committee of councilors came out to LA and met at Occidental to structure our final draft of the CUR strategic plan for opening to national membership and creating a national office. We wanted to put it forward at the University of Richmond CUR meeting. My husband Mike, as a chemist, was very comfortable going out to dinner with us and enjoyed getting to know the councilors about whom he had heard a great deal.

That was the first time I realized that although Mike was shy, he was much more outgoing over a dinner than at a stand-up party. He once told me that at big parties, he might as well have a lampshade over his head.

I presented our strategic plan at the meeting of all the CUR

Councilors in Richmond, and it was accepted by the Council. We opened membership to all comers while I was president of CUR. Instead of little conferences with just councilors present, we started having huge annual meetings of our membership. Now our constituency included not only those successful at undergraduate research, but also those who wanted to start it up at their campuses. We raised money to start a national office, hired John Stevens of UNC Asheville as the first executive officer, raised additional endowment, started an April Dialogue for CUR members to visit with NIH and NSF program officers in the spring, and began to have outstanding undergraduate students present posters on the Hill for Congressional viewing.

We raised money for an internship program honoring the brightest and best science students at predominantly undergraduate schools. A lot of the good ideas in those years came from Mike Doyle, then at Trinity University in Texas and Stuart Crampton at Williams. I thought up the April Dialogue, the spring visit to the funding agencies in DC, and personally visited a lot of those we asked to speak the first time we had the meeting. I asked NIH to host the event, and they did a great job for CUR. I also had the fun of planning one of the CUR national meetings along with Jim Gentile, whose Hope College was going to be the meeting site.

Interestingly, Scott Pyron, who had asked if the four biology councilors were ready for national leadership, asked me another important question later on in my career. I was on sabbatical at CalTech in Leroy Hood's laboratory, and Scott was visiting in town and invited me to lunch. When we got to the restaurant, he asked me, "Laura, why apply to Research Corporation for funding? Your projects are worthy of support at a larger scale by the federal agencies, and you should know that. Don't compete with those just getting started or unable to do such interesting work." I was stunned.

I had thought we were going to reminisce about the glories of CUR, and didn't expect to be spurred into action. But, almost immediately I applied for an NIH AREA grant and received it. I had become too discouraged by my first NIH rejection, and rejections of four other NIH and NSF attempts following that. I hadn't tried again since we had published several studies and been well into our next project. It meant a lot to me, in retrospect, that he let me know that my work was strong enough to go back to the competition.

Another unanticipated outcome of the CUR involvement brought me back into the orbit of Peter Stanley. He had gone from Carleton to the Ford Foundation, and then moved on to be President at Pomona College. It was just down the road from Oxy, but on another plane entirely. Pomona was in the top five liberal arts colleges nationally but Oxy felt good when it made it into the top twenty-five. I ended up taking the position of Academic Vice President and Dean of the College at Pomona College under Peter Stanley's leadership. One of the principal features of my record that attracted Pomona to me as a candidate was the CUR national presidency, along with my strategic planning and fund raising with CUR.

CUR really had a resounding impact in my life, making the final answer to Scott's original question, about a national leadership role, a decided, "Yes!" I had to be ready to take on a national leadership role advocating for the value of undergraduate research because there was a vacuum. I turned out to be much better prepared to take it up than I had thought. In turn, that choice rebounded in my life's trajectory taking me to places I would have never imagined I could go. I value undergraduate research so much myself, and am so convinced that it's the best possible learning experience for my students, that my success as an advocate for it is a highlight of my life.

CHAPTER 20
HEATHER GOES FROM NURSERY SCHOOL
TO COLLEGE IN ONE DAY

One of the joys of my life has been watching my children grow and develop, but parenthood and career were not easy to manage in tandem. I will describe one of those times of role conflict for you, from a time when my daughter Heather was in preschool.

"Mommy, I'm dizzy," Heather says, very soft and weak.

"I know, I'm sorry honey. I'm going to get someone take care of you." I hope. I call two older women who sometimes can baby sit sick kids, but both are already busy. Mike has long since gone to work. I have a lecture in Molecular Genetics in an hour, and it will take about 30 minutes to get there and get organized.

"Heather, are you sure you can't go to Montessori school today?" She loves her main teacher Sherani and her sometimes-teacher Joann.

"I can't see Joann today, Mommy. I'm sick." Her voice is like a distant echo. I feel her forehead; it is warmer than usual.

"Does your tummy hurt? Does your throat hurt?"

"My tummy." What can I do? I have missed several classes for these students already.

"Heather, could you go to school with me and take a nap in your sleeping bag while I talk to the students?"

"Maybe." Not a good option either, but the students in this

class have a test in one week, and they need to have good, solid knowledge about how information moves from the genes into proteins.

"I'm going out to the garage to get your sleeping bag." Even though we have recently moved to a larger house, where she has her own room, storage is tight and we keep the camping equipment in the garage.

"Okay, Mommy," she sighs softly. I go out and get the sleeping bag and the roll up mattress and put them in the car. Then I go back to her. "How are you, Heather?"

"I'm so sick I feel like a sock," she says. "What kind of a sock?"

"An old soft sock with no stuffing," she says. I'm sorry to have to ask her to move at all. I call the HMO to which we belong and get an appointment at 4:30PM.

"You're so lucky," the woman carols, "you got the last appointment today!" But my child is sick and that's hours later and...I couldn't bring her right away even if she offered me an appointment. So, let's go to school. I put my briefcase into the car.

Then, I say, "Heather, I need you to get up and walk out to the car. I'm bringing you a bottle of water, and you can take your blanket."

"OK, Mommy," she says, but she's very shaky and has to lean hard on me on the way out. I buckle her into the back seat and kiss her forehead. "I love you, Mommy," she says.

"I love you too, Heather," I say. But do I love her enough? Why am I putting my students' needs above hers?

Heather sleeps almost all the way to Occidental College. We drive right past her Montessori school, where she's known as "The earthworm" because she loves to dig in the dirt. It's an affectionate name as best I can tell. Otherwise, I would object. She doesn't mind it, as long as she can dig! That's just as well, since the older kids who study in the Geodesic Dome across the street come over after school and use all the swings and climbing equipment. They're known as "The Dome Kids" and there's not much affection in that soubriquet. There's a scorpion tail twist in the tone of voice when kids Heather's age say the name. She doesn't stir as we drive by, and I let her sleep.

Finally we get to Occidental.

She moans a little as I tell her, "Heather, I need to take you in now. We will go to my office and you can sleep on the floor for a while." I help her walk, carrying my briefcase and her sleeping bag and mattress. I roll them out on the floor of my office.

She says, "I'm going to sleep now, okay Mommy?"

"Yes, H-ee, go ahead and take a nap. Later I will have to move you to my class room, but it's good to sleep now." She spells her name, "H-e-h-e-h-e-R!" so her nickname is H-ee (say the letter name, and then add the ee). "I love you Mommy," she says. She's already asleep.

I remember when she was first born. My son Lyle, by my first husband, was 11 years old and was staying with my friend Cecilia while my second husband Mike helped me though labor and delivery. It took almost 24 hours. Mike had never had a child before, and the Kaiser hospital allowed us to have a "bonding period" after she was born when we just cuddled her for an hour before they took her off for whatever hospitals do with babies. Mike is six feet four and was covered from head to toe in a green surgical outfit that he had put on at the nurses' request. He took Heather when they handed her to him, and he had a beatific expression on his face. Big Mike holding tiny Heather. I will never forget how they looked, and the feeling of tiny, dependent mortality that we loved dearly. Heather was just that lovable and dependent at this moment; was I failing her? I worried. I collected the materials for the class, notes I had made the day before, a model that I wanted to use to demonstrate how the molecules interact, a package of graded quizzes to return.

It's time to go to class.

"Heather, I need to take you to my class now, but you can sleep there if you want to." She moans a little bit, but rouses enough to help me help her walk along to the classroom, which is down stairs and down a long hall. It has never seemed so long before, but today it stretches for miles. But, she's able to keep walking slowly.

"Do you want to get a drink at the water fountain?" I ask.

It's one of her favorite activities at my school, but today she says, "No, Mommy, I have my water bottle." Her voice is tiny, without its usual lively resonance. I worry more.

We spread out her sleeping bag on its mattress right next to the big lecture desk, with its shiny black top. Usually, she asks to draw on the blackboard with chalk if we're in this room, but today, she lies down with a soft sigh, and goes back to sleep almost instantly. I lay out my materials for class. Here is the first student.

"Hello, Wei, how are you today?" I say.

"Fine, but it looks like your daughter isn't. Is she sick?" he asks. Each student goes through the same ritual when he or she arrives. I wonder if they're all thinking I'm an ogre to put Heather through this. But, I'm here now. I hope they can concentrate.

"I'm sorry, class, but as you know Heather is sick. I'll try not to wake her up; she can't go to the doctor until late this afternoon. So, the best thing for her is to sleep, and I couldn't get a baby sitter for her today. But, since I knew you needed to prepare for your next test, I felt like I had to come." I continued with the lecture, "Here's a model of RNA polymerase sticking to DNA. It's starting to transcribe messenger RNA, a disposable copy of the gene that can be translated into protein."

I continue with the lecture, and along the way, Heather wakes up and asks, "Are you going to step on me, Mommy?" The class gasps.

"No, honey, I'm being very careful not to step on you." I tell her.

But she looks concerned. Her sunken eyes follow me as I move around behind the desk. She rolls over inside the sleeping bag, trying to get to a safer spot. I finish the lecture in record time, about ten minutes early. This early ending happens partly because the students don't ask any questions, probably out of fear that they're prolonging Heather's ordeal.

I tell them, "OK, you have a gift of time now. I know you probably had questions you didn't ask, but I'm grateful to be able to take Heather home until her appointment. So, please email me your questions and I'll respond as soon as I can. I'll also start the next class with a question period so you can be sure you clearly understand this material."

They say goodbye and leave, most of them saying goodbye to Heather too, who is wide awake but not very lively.

I say, "Heather, we can go home now."

She says, "Thank you, Mommy." I wonder if she will remember this in future years, maybe think she "went to college" when she was only five years old. We walk out to the car with our piles of belongings, and get in. Heather goes to sleep immediately. We drive home, and walk inside slowly. She goes back to bed, and sleeps until 1:00 PM, when she drinks a whole glass of water. That's a surprise because she almost never finishes a drink, and still today leaves about half the diet coke in each can she opens.

"I'm not hungry Mommy," she tells me when I ask if she wants any food. I give her some baby pain medicine in a liquid form because she claims she cannot swallow pills. Probably it's hard for her because her tonsils are like golf balls most of the time. She goes back to bed until time for the doctor visit.

We go to the HMO office to see the doctor and have to stand in line to check in. I have Heather sit in a chair while I meander slowly through the line. She almost goes to sleep while I work my way up to the check-in position. After check in, I take her down the hall to the waiting room for her pediatrician, who is mercifully able to see her. Heather doesn't take well to strange doctors.

"How's my sunshine girl today?" she asks Heather. She tries to smile, but says, "It's raining."

"Oh, no." The doctor, with a wonderful bedside manner, goes through her usual routine and finds that Heather has an ear infection, tonsillitis, and probably a mild flu.

"She should stay home for three days and take these antibiotics for the tonsils and ear infection," she tells me. I'm pleased to see she has prescribed a liquid that Heather actually doesn't hate. It's pink, gooey Amoxicillin. I'm also guiltily pleased that she could be through the recovery period before my next class meets. So, we pick up the medicine in the pharmacy and go home.

Today I look back on this day from time to time, because Heather says, "Mom, do you remember that day you took me to class when I was sick? And I was on the floor near your feet while you talked? And I thought you might step on me?"

I think it's some kind of an iconic experience of being the daughter of a working professor. She was with me, but she had to go to work with me for that to happen. Or, she was only with me because I couldn't get a baby sitter. Or, she was with me but scared I might step on her. All of the above.

My children are very precious to me, and I learned more from them than from any other source I can think of, but at the same time, they were a very deep well of guilt that I plumbed from time to time as they grew up. This day was one of the sources of that guilt for years afterwards.

At Oxy I once appeared on a panel with three others talking about families and careers. We each gave prepared statements about having kids and a career. Each student there heard a positive gloss on "having it all." Most of our listeners were women who would think about these issues in a personal way. Each of us women professors with children was reduced to tears by at least one of the students' questions. My stinger was, "Dr Mays, have you ever had to do something for your career that you think made you sacrifice your child's happiness?" I knew the answer. But I burst into tears. My son always had his birthday parties postponed by my attendance at a National Science Foundation Graduate Fellowships panel. I was too choked up to explain my tears then. I had to tell the girl who asked me that after the panel was over.

I once read in a novel that kids are "hostages to fortune". That's part of it, but it's also the idea that in another age or culture, you and your child could be as inseparable after birth as before, for a good long time. With Heather, I was able to manage a bit over a year before returning to work. With Lyle, it was one week. How painful that was!

But I cannot say I regret having kids for a minute. Never was there a more wonderful slice of life to enjoy, find exasperating, see change in, play with, and become close to. It raises unanswerable questions to people like me. Would I be as good a mother if I didn't work, or would I rage at the kids because I would blame them for my lack of mental activity? Would I be as interested in their achievements if I weren't reading about the progression of others? Isn't the college professor career benign for a mother, having the option of working at home when you want? How could I leave full time, highly competitive research in molecular biology and have it stand still for me and be waiting intact when I returned? The guilt remains. Would I step on her? Never on purpose.

CHAPTER 21
LYLE CHOOSES HIS OWN ROAD

With my son Lyle, the issues I had to deal with often were based in racism, I'm sorry to say. I'd like to take you along to one of Lyle's schools as I tried to fix a bad situation he fell into during junior high school.

I'm sitting across from my son Lyle's teacher. He goes to Eliot Junior High, also known as the pink prison, since it's a huge complex of pink sandstone buildings full of young teenagers under what amounts to martial law.

"Don't worry, I understand that it's just too hard for him," she says. I've heard from Lyle that this woman has no control over her class. Last week the students threw a desk out of her second story classroom during class. I have no idea what hackles are, but if I had them they rose.

"Do you think he can't understand English?" I asked incredulously. We're conferring because he's making an F in this class.

"Well, I know it's hard for these kids, with their racial background and all," she drawls. Okay, I'm white and he's black. And this teacher has been recruited from the South because no one from here would want to work at Eliot. But, really, in this day and age, haven't the teachers been inculcated with "Stand and Deliver" mentality? Don't they realize the cost of low expectations is to get what you predict?

"Well, you might want to look at his English aptitude scores," I say, after giving myself time to calm down a little and decide how to approach her.

His teacher thumbs clumsily through Lyle's file, looking for the chart from his last series of tests. She opens his file and pages through it. She raises her eyes to meet mine with a look of complete astonishment.

"Well my goodness, he made in the 98th percentile in English aptitude," she said. I see her wheels turning, wondering if it would cost her more to assume he had cheated somehow on the standardized tests or that he might be smart and she wasn't reaching him.

"I can get him a tutor," she says finally.

"OK, please do, because he can certainly do the work if he puts his mind to it," I say, with no real expectations. I wonder how things have gone so badly for Lyle and worry that he is on a slippery slope towards failure. I also have a momentary pang of pain for this young woman who came here to try to help but who lacks the first tool she needs: being convinced the students can learn.

I flash back to sixth grade at Altadena School, when Lyle entered the Pasadena School District's writing contest. He had no trouble retaining reams of information about sports, and could recite sports statistics with the best of them. So, he sat in the library at the designated time and he wrote a long essay about the sporting achievements of Michael Jordan for his timed essay without sources. The essay was crammed with details, embellished with lively anecdotes, funny and delightful.

The district sent someone out to the school, convinced that he couldn't have written this essay, or if he did, he had cheated by having a sports almanac under the table. They made him sit in the library and write as close a facsimile as possible while the inspector watched him. He received the writing award. But the award could never take away the taste of being doubted that strongly. That shame will last forever, for him and for me, and probably for his teachers and classmates as well.

I was appalled partly because Lyle would never cheat in school; he didn't even want help on his homework unless of the most Socratic method. If there was ever a "Mother please, I want to do it myself" kid, it was Lyle. He was diagnosed as gifted early. Ironically, that meant that his skills were somewhat weak because he and the other GATE kids were diverted into enrichment classes at the times when he might have honed his skills at English or math.

"He's gifted, not born with knowledge," I protested to his teachers, but the GATE program required that he go and the times he went weren't at the discretion of me or his teachers.

"Too bad, he could have used the English practice," they told me.

Lyle loved to create new ideas, loved to debate positions and find out all of your best arguments. I've had colleagues from universities elsewhere who visited LA, came to dinner at our house, and later wrote saying they couldn't believe he was only whatever age he was, and rave about how much they had enjoyed talking with him. Yet he would leave Eliot Junior High School convinced that he was stupid and that no black student would ever be smart. What a waste, I thought.

During that same time period at Eliot, he began to be "sick" for days in a row. I asked him why, and he said that people had threatened to kill him, or to beat him up on the way home. I was furious. I called the school and demanded that they do something.

The counselor said, "No, he might be scared but nothing would really happen. We can't do anything anyway, unless something would happen on the school grounds."

I thought about picking him up every day, but when I was teaching afternoon labs it just wasn't possible. Mike was biking to and from work. I couldn't afford taxis for Lyle. Eliot Junior High was only six blocks from our house. I was worried sick.

One way Lyle coped was to stay after school and play basketball until I could come to pick him up around 5:30. There were always plenty of boys who wanted to play, and evidently they weren't all that gang-infested compared to others at that school. He became good at basketball. He also played in a night league at the Boys' Club. Mike and I told him he had to keep his grades at passing level to do that. He did, but only barely at times. His grades through elementary school had been very strong, but it wasn't cool to be smart at his junior high school, and he had to be cool.

I was at home on a Saturday, putting a hem back into one of Heather's little dresses, when I heard the phone ring in the kitchen. I walked past the TV with Lyle sprawled in front of it piling up blocks for Heather to knock down, and answered it.

"Hello, Laura, I just wanted to talk with you about Lyle," said the voice. "This is Fran from church. I'm the admissions dean at Flintridge Prep."

A long silence happened while I got my shocked brain collected together again. "Hello, Fran, what can I do for you?" I hoped that was non-committal enough to cover whatever she might want.

"Well, he applied and took the placement examination for high school here. You know the coach liked the way he played basketball and has been recruiting him along with his friend Hank. He wrote this amazing essay for us about how he wanted and needed to get into an environment where it was cool to learn, where peer pressure would be in the right direction instead of leading downwards to trouble with the law. We loved the essay.

But Laura, we almost never admit anyone whose grades range from A to D-. It would really be a first."

Another long silence while I coped with this shock. Lyle had applied. Lyle had taken the placement exam for this preparatory high school. Lyle had said nothing, perhaps wanting to be sure it was possible first. What should I do?

Don't say you didn't know, I decided. "Well I'm glad you liked his essay. I'm sure it was from his best thoughts, because Eliot has been so bad for him academically," I said. "He did much better all through elementary school."

"Hmm, I don't know what to do," said Fran. "Has he ever taken an intelligence test?"

"As it happens, he took two. Once when he was tested for admission to Polytechnic for kindergarten, and once at Noyes School," I said, suddenly seeing a ray of hope. He had done very well on both, testing above 140 each time.

"Well, I will ask him to have those scores sent over, then, and maybe that will mitigate the grades a bit. Was he admitted to Poly?"

Wow, I had pushed the right button this time without knowing it. Poly is the giant gorilla among prep schools in Pasadena. "Yes, he was and he attended kindergarten there," I said. I didn't tell her that two thirds of the way through the year he had asked me, "Why are there only two black kids in every class, one boy and one girl?" Richard, who might have been unmoved by Lyle's observation because the academics were so strong there, had really wanted him to go to Poly. But I was horrified because he had experienced such a good multicultural environment at Pacific Oaks preschool. So that was the only year he went there.

I went back into the living room and said, "Lyle, can we talk?"

He made a mother-must-we face but agreed. We went outside to the picnic table on the patio and sat down.

"Lyle, that was Fran, and she wanted to talk with me about

your application to Flintridge Prep," I told him. "Can you tell me about that?"

"I was waiting until I knew something," he said defensively.

"What do you think?" I asked. "Would that be a good school for you?"

"Mom, you know it would. Anything would be better than Muir." Muir was the local high school, where those graduating from Eliot junior high typically matriculated. It was possible to get a good education there, but there were lots of problems with gangs.

"What have they told you about money?" I asked him.

"Coach said that if I'm qualified, they will meet my needs so I can still afford to go to college," he said.

Suddenly I saw that this move might really be possible. We had saved a lot of funds from Richard's social security to pay for Lyle's college education, and I was worried about depleting it through prep school. But, he might not even survive until time to go to college if he went to Muir, given his problems at Eliot. So, I was pleased and told Lyle I was proud of him.

He looked embarrassed and said, "Oh, Mom, I had to do it." But of course he didn't. He had just taken charge of his own life, and he had done a great job of it. No compulsion, no inevitability about it. He drifted back into the living room and I sat there glowing with pride for about 20 minutes, and then called Mike to tell him. I think he had the same reaction.

"I feel like we just won the lottery," he said. No, I thought, winning the lottery couldn't possibly feel this good. It was better than an NIH grant, better than a publication in the most important journal in molecular biology, the best it could possibly be.

CHAPTER 22
OUTREACH TO HIGH SCHOOLS THROUGH TOPS

There are times when you do what needs to be done and don't count the cost. Often the efforts you make in those times bear fruit beyond your wildest dreams. I want to tell you about a very rewarding project like that, TOPS.

When I arrived to review its biology department, Juniata College in the backwoods of Pennsylvania was snowed in, not with snow but with ruby and citrine leaves. With every walk between buildings, I enjoyed the fall feelings I had missed for so long, living in California. The crackling crisp sound of dry leaves underfoot, the bright colors and beautifully shaped edges of the leaves, the patterned swirls of leaves moving on the breezes were all welcome reminders of how much I had once loved autumn.

My meetings with biologists, their staff, and the administrators were done, and I was about to take my yellow pad of notes and depart when I met a chemist who was going to change my life. Don was supposed to chat with me about the relationship between chemistry and biology, but somehow we started talking about "Science in Motion," the high school outreach program that Juniata, under his leadership, had undertaken. They had an NSF grant and had obtained equipment for today's chemistry. Juniata ran summer workshops for high school teachers, and those who attended and practiced with the equipment could use it free of charge during the academic year.

When I got back to Oxy, I talked with my friend Chris Craney. He and I were the entire biochemistry faculty; he replaced the retired Jack McAnally. I told him about the Juniata program, mentioning that Don had said he could come out and give a talk about it if we were interested. Chris and I had no time; we were overwhelmed with work. There was no way we could even think about starting a new program. But the idea of this one was compelling. I don't think I have ever learned, and probably won't, that something that needs doing is more than I can take on, and neither has Chris.

"You know how they're always cutting the lab budget in LA high schools," Chris said. "Would this just give them permission to cut more?"

"Maybe, but at least the kids could learn some decent current science," I said. "Yes, you know sciences are competing for students with economics, with the great computer labs for econ that all the high schools have. All the science labs have are a few pipets and maybe one old Spec 20."

"Yes," I said, "and all the experiments they do are right out of the AP book, not at all investigational."

With that, we let the subject drop, but we returned to it every week or two. "Why don't we invite him out?" Chris asked.

"OK, who would we ask to hear him?"

"What about high school teachers we know, because they're Oxy grads or for any other reasons," Chris suggested.

"I wonder how many that would be?"

Chris, who is really quick with numbers, thought for only a second and said, "Maybe around 50-60."

"An evening event in the bio palace then?" I asked. The Biology Department had just moved into a lovely new building with an auditorium that would fit a crowd that size comfortably.

"Good, so let's get to work. Can you contact Don and get

dates? And I'll get together lists of high school teachers," Chris said.

On the night of the talk, Don was calm and confident. We had a good crowd of 60 high school science teachers who taught biology, chemistry, or both. Don started by telling the story of his program. He emphasized throughout the role that the teachers had in designing what was done, choosing the equipment, and after the first summer, in teaching most of the classes. He had hired one of the high school teachers to serve as a coordinator for his program. He told the audience that he and the other Juniata professors considered themselves catalysts of the program rather than saviors bringing the word to the teachers. The audience applauded vigorously at the end, and immediately surrounded Chris and me wanting to know if we were going to do something similar. We put a sign-up sheet out and twenty-five interested teachers left us their contact information.

I told Mike and Lyle about the idea of a science outreach program to LA schools over dinner, and they both thought it sounded good. Lyle had thought then that he would become a sports legend (in basketball or maybe as a football running back), and would start up a sort of boys and girls club to support after-school academics in downtown LA when he was rich and famous. He said this was a step in that direction, and anything to upgrade the poor learning experience in the LA schools was a great idea.

Mike was quieter; as usual Lyle had jumped in a breath before Mike had thought through what he wanted to say. But when Lyle slacked off, Mike said, "It does sound like a good idea. But don't you need someone to help the teachers when you deliver the equipment to the schools? How can they remember an experiment they learned during the summer when they are overwhelmed with work during the school year?"

"You're right, we need to hire someone to go with the van and equipment who could refresh the teachers. Don has a person like that," I said. I could see that he was really excited by this idea. I recalled that he finished his qualifying examinations for the PhD in plant biochemistry at University of Georgia and dropped out, thinking he liked teaching much more than research. After that, he took education courses at Bowie State in Laurel, MD. In fact, a nun whose tape had graced our wedding, had been one of his teachers in that program. I saw that his eyes were glowing as he thought about teaching. But then he worked at USC Medical School in the endocrinology laboratories, doing medical research, so he had no chance to teach except informally. Later on, he moved into industry, but in 2007, he has been called to the ministry and started divinity school. He may end up teaching yet.

About a month after Don's talk, Chris and I still hadn't done anything about starting an outreach program. We had both agreed to go to Bethesda, MD for the National Institutes of Health conference for the AREA program (Academic Research Enhancement Awards). That program had funded each of our research labs.

"Let's sit together on the way back from NIH and scope out what we have to do to make this high school outreach happen," Chris suggested.

"Okay, do we need to bring grant proposal guidelines?"

"Sure, but we don't have to be focused on that stuff. Let's just blue sky what we want, and worry about how to pay for it later."

The first thing we decided on the flight was to start with the bottom line: GTO or Give Teachers Ownership. We didn't want to design what we thought they needed, but instead we wanted to get teachers involved in designing what they thought they would need as experiments and equipment, for the classes they were teaching.

Our general idea was similar to Don's at Juniata. We would somehow get a truck or van, stock it with equipment and supplies for the experiments the teachers wanted to do, and let them book deliveries of it to their classrooms. Although NSF didn't have a program that would help us buy the truck and the equipment, we thought the Oxy Development office, which was used to working with Chris, would probably help us get those things. Oxy had a lot of teacher alumni/ae who could potentially participate in the program.

We decided to start meeting with as many of the teachers as we could get together after we returned. The teachers needed to begin tentative plans for the experiments and equipment because Chris and I needed those ideas to get funding from the Teacher Enhancement Program at NSF. The grant would pay for stipends for the teachers who took the summer workshops, supplies, and a small stipend to us for teaching the workshops.

The greater part of the NSF grant money we would need for hiring two people: a part time administrative assistant to book the van deliveries, check things in and out, and keep the effort organized and a full time high school resource teacher who would work at Oxy, and go with each delivery to serve as a backup to the teacher requesting the van. He or she would get to know other high school teachers and help us recruit interested workshop/van participants.

Chris and I and Eleanor, a wonderful secondary education specialist from the Oxy education department, along with Grace Quimbita, a teaching postdoctoral fellow in Chemistry, started meeting monthly to discuss our plans. We met with the teacher volunteers three times to talk about what kinds of experiments might be interesting to them. The teachers defined the needs and desires and we stuck to the ways and means.

The team came up with a set of four experiments, each using a different kind of exciting state-of-the-art equipment with marvelous computer displays of the data. My pet experiment was growing two cultures of yeast with and without a lot of aeration in liquid (sort of like making beer badly and well). Then, the students removed the yeast cells and tested the liquid for alcohol using high pressure liquid chromatography. The equipment we wanted to use, and eventually got, was a flashy modern Hewlett Packard HPLC with a big diode array detector run by a color-screen computer. We put the whole shebang on a wheeled cart that could be rolled onto a truck and chained into place for the trip to its destination.

We planned other experiments with plant pigments, protein separations, and DNA fragmentation. The participants, even without our urging, seemed to gravitate to our forte: biochemistry, the interface between our two fields. We recruited expert faculty members to consult on each of the planned experiments. We wrote our proposal, got it signed by the administration (even the offer to have Development help us raise the funds for the van and equipment), and sent it off to the National Science Foundation.

Meanwhile, Mike was still riding his bicycle back and forth to USC in downtown LA from our home in Altadena, about seven miles away. He was in great physical shape, but he had to ride up a three mile steep hill (Lake Avenue, Pasadena) at the end of the trip. It was very smoggy then, so I was worried about him. Finally, we were able to afford a used car that he could use on bad air days.

The NSF Teacher Enhancement Program loved our proposal. Of course, once we were approved and funded, we had to put the program in place. We recruited a steering committee of some of our most faithful teachers from the planning process, and began to advertise for a full time teacher for the van.

I was really dubious that someone would give up the great perks of LAUSD to do this project for two years on soft money, but I reckoned without the science teacher shortage. We had quite a few strong applicants, mostly convinced that they could get a two year unpaid leave from LAUSD to do this and then return with full rights and privileges. The great teacher we hired got exactly this deal, much to our delight.

We were also lucky enough to hire as our part time coordinator, a calm, smiling, efficient person who is still with the program over ten years later. She proved to be completely unflappable, although her limits have been severely tested.

The first summer, we ran the workshops in teaching labs in the Bio palace, with several other Oxy faculty joining Chris and me as mentors of the teacher-participants. All participants got notebooks filled with background science briefings, handouts they could use for the experiment, and predicted results, along with space for their own results and the notes on our discussions. Most of those teachers were among those who heard Don and had been involved from the start. They did a great job with the background and the laboratory work and were very enthusiastic about using these experiments in their classes the following year. Mike, a teacher at Arcadia High School, signed up to use the yeast experiment I was mentoring.

Chris had told me about the weak science budgets, but Mike really opened my eyes. He told me that the science division at his school had only $1000 in supply funds for laboratories for all the classes for the entire year. And Arcadia was by no means a poor area. Our experiments weren't just going to upgrade the science labs a notch, they were going to jump them several orders of magnitude in sophistication and expense.

Mike and other participants requested that Chris and I visit the high schools as our time permitted and meet with the administrators to try to get more funding for science labs. They welcomed our program, which we called Teachers + Occidental Partnerships in Science (TOPS), but they didn't expect it would last forever and worried about future science funding.

The first time I visited a campus using the TOPS experiments was at Mike's school, Arcadia High. He had invited both Chris and me to come, meet with his principal, and visit some of his classes using the yeast experiment with the big, flashy HPLC. We found that the administrators were excited about our program, supportive of Mike, but said that they had little discretion over funding. However, we heard later that at every school we visited, the science lab budget increased substantially the following year.

The class I recall best was Mike's class for students who were disinterested in science and just trying to fulfill a requirement. The students kept asking us, "This ethanol. Do you mean it's alcohol? Are we really making alcohol? How pure is it?"

We explained that what their experiment was quite similar to making beer, and that it was important to keep the yeast from using air or they would forego making alcohol and just burn up the sugar.

"Cool!" said one student, complete with tattoo and nose ring. "At last we learn something I wanna know!"

The experiment called for injecting the product expected to be ethanol into a High Pressure Liquid Chromatograph (HPLC). It separated the mixture into peaks that showed up in different colors on the TV-like monitor, and the students could print out the results. They could inject pure ethanol and compare it with what the yeast had made. The peak from the known alcohol and the yeast product should appear at the same number of minutes after injection.

That day, I feared that shooting the yeast product into the HPLC might seem superfluous to the students after our discussion, but it wasn't. The display was multicolor and live action; you could see exactly when a compound was coming out of the column and how much of it was there. In the experiment, the students made a standard curve by shooting different concentrations of alcohol into the HPLC column and watching different sizes of peaks come out. The computer automatically integrated the peaks and gave them a number that they could plot against the amount they thought they had shot into the column, making a graph.

Then they shot in their yeast products or brews, one from yeast with air and oxygen, and the other from yeast without air. The prediction was that the ones without air should have made alcohol, but not the ones with air. In fact, both had made some alcohol, but the one without air had a lot bigger alcohol peak than the one with oxygen.

Using the standard curve graph, they could see exactly how much each culture had made. Their prediction of more in the airless culture was vindicated, and boy, were they excited. I suppose it had been a crap-shoot whether or not experiments had worked in the past, and they weren't expecting much. But they got more than they expected this time.

The colors, the moving cursor, and the 'shot needle' aspects of this analysis attracted the students. Several seemed very good at the steps needed. Mike said he had never seen the students from this particular class so engaged in what they were doing. We were beyond pleased with what we had seen, and went back to Oxy invigorated to raise more money through Development for this project.

Sadly, the alcohol's relevance to my own life was about to kick in. My husband Mike had a bike wreck on Lincoln Avenue going down to get my car back from the dealer where it was being serviced. On my way home in his car, I picked up Heather and we were almost through dinner when the doorbell rang. Two policemen were there with a mangled bike: mine. Mike had borrowed it rather than using his for some reason, and although he always insisted on bike helmets, that time he hadn't been wearing one. The policemen told us that Mike was at Huntington Hospital emergency room. The bike looked so crumpled that I was terrified for his life. We jumped in the car and rushed down to the hospital. He was on an IV, a bit bloody and battered looking.

The ER doctor pulled me aside and told me, "He was totally stone drunk. Never should have been riding out in traffic in that state. Does he know about Alcoholic Anonymous?"

I told him Mike didn't have an alcohol problem generally. He looked skeptical. Mike was there for a while, and that doctor left. His successor was a black doctor who chatted with me. When he found I was an Oxy professor of biology, he told me he knew Kevin, one of my favorite black premeds from Oxy who had gone into emergency medicine.

I brushed off the incident with Mike's bicycle wreck; thought it was just an accident and would never happen again. Instead, as our lives unwound, it proved to be a straw in the wind. Mike was a very quiet drunk. He went into his area of our house and drank massive quantities of scotch that he kept squirreled away there without my knowing about it. We had a liquor cabinet in the dining area that he never used except for company liqueurs. But it was years later when I faced his alcohol problems. At the time, I just shrugged and thought it was bad luck that he had been drunk when he needed to be en route somewhere.

Teachers + Occidental Partnerships in Science, or TOPS, is a special highlight in my life. Over the years I have done a lot of things, in science, in CUR, for the National Science Foundation, for the other societies, and for Occidental and Pomona Colleges. I have never done anything of which I'm prouder than helping Chris start up the TOPS program. It's wonderful that more than ten years after I left Oxy, TOPS is still operating and helping LA science students get excited about biochemistry. I get a warm glow whenever I open my page at the National Science Foundation Fastlane grants management web page and see TOPS listed.

CHAPTER 23
MY GENOMICS SABBATICAL

On my second sabbatical leave from Occidental, my family members weren't mobile so I looked for an exciting opportunity in Los Angeles. Now let me tell you about my first encounter with genomics, when I was on sabbatical at Caltech.

It was 7:30 at night in 1986. Even though I was on sabbatical leave, supposedly not teaching, I was at a church in East Pasadena to talk to a group of senior citizens attending a lecture series on new vistas in science. A retired Oxy professor put together this "cutting edge science" series.

"Think about making the news understandable, and about policy issues," he told me. "We aren't going to be doing any experiments, so the details are less important."

My assignment was how genes act, viewed at the level of molecules. I thought hard about what to present and decided that as voters, the seniors of Pasadena would like to know about the 'human genome project', the idea that the government should fund a project to obtain the sequence of every one of the human genes. It was of particular interest to me then, since I was working at Cal Tech under the auspices of Leroy Hood, a top tier scientist studying genes for immunity. I started with the nature of the gene, showed how it can be inherited and how it can be expressed, that all the genes together make up the genome, and then went into

189

future directions:

"If we could do without one aircraft carrier, then we could afford to sequence the whole human genome," I said. Lee Hood thought it could even cost less than a carrier, because he predicted, and planned to contribute towards, a great improvement in the methods for DNA sequencing that would make it less costly.

"What can we get if we sequence the human genome?" I continued. "We may be able to find the basis for a lot of human medical conditions. If we do, then new treatments can be found. We may find out the secret of why we cannot grow a new arm or leg as a salamander could. We may be able to take stem cells into the laboratory and grow new skin, new retinas, new liver lobes. 'Personalized medicine,' medical treatment that takes into account how you might react to different medicines, can become a reality when we can sequence each person's DNA."

I felt like I was winging it, shooting the moon, exaggerating the potential.

After my talk, I was surrounded by bright-eyed, excited senior citizens who wanted to tell me that they favored the sequencing.

"We're getting together and writing to our congressmen telling them to forget the next aircraft carrier, but to sequence the human genome instead," an especially articulate woman told me.

"Thank you for letting us know about this while we can do something to help it happen," another said.

I felt that in a small way, these letters might make the difference in getting the project to fly. It would be a lot more significant than one more aircraft carrier, I thought.

The following day I was in lab early, excited about my research, wanting to make the most of my time.

"Hello, Laura. How are your transgenic mice?"

I jumped and turned to find Leroy Hood. I worked under his research associate, Iwona Stroynowski, now a professor at

University of Texas Southwestern Medical Center. I had become fascinated with the new ideas called "systems biology." We scientists were just beginning to see that when you take apart the cell down to the minutia of the universe, you have to reconnect molecules and watch how they work together to make any sense out of what the cell actually does. There is an almost Buddhist feeling to this concept: go too far in one direction and a self-correction is inevitable.

"We have injected the mouse eggs with our gene, and we hope to have transgenic mice next week." I answer him. "When did you get back?"

Lee spent a large part of his time on the road, talking at various academic and research centers, site-visiting labs for governmental funding agencies, and attending meetings of groups trying to address problems in molecular biology, collecting information pollen along the way.

"About midnight. The lab was full then. Where is everybody?"

"I don't know. It's usually pretty quiet in early morning around here. I think people prefer to work at night."

Many people in the lab thought Lee never slept. The grapevine said he might appear in the lab at any hour of day or night, bright eyed and ready to discuss science with anyone present. I was prepared to believe it.

"What do people out there think about sequencing the human genome?" I asked. As he traveled around the country, Lee was trying to drum up enthusiasm for investing the nation's scientific support funds into finding out the sequence of the human genome.

Lee said, "Not as much interest as I had hoped. I think a problem with getting people on board is that the Department of Energy is the sponsor, rather than the National Institute of Health. People think it shouldn't be the DOE, even though it's their idea and they have done a lot of the planning for the project."

"Why do they care?" I asked.

Lee leaned on the lab bench next to my work table.

"It's both prestige and money, I think. People look up to NIH and they're used to getting grants from them, so they don't want to have to learn the house politics for another funding agency." He shrugged. "The nay-sayers can't stop it, though. Lots of momentum is building up. I'm going to testify before Congress next month."

"Will they try to restructure where the funding comes from?" Lee thought it over, pulling on an ear lobe.

"Maybe. That will take a fight, though. Probably NIH would win that one; Congress is full of people who need great health research and love NIH."

Lee stood up straight. "Come down and show me your data later," he said. "You've put your gene into several different cell lines, right?"

"Yes, I have, and I will," I said.

He walked away and started down the corridor, looking for more people. I heard his footsteps pause. He was probably looking at the white board in the hall where there was a joking list to which every passing person contributed. It was entitled "Whose DNA should we sequence?" We wrote, "a male astronaut," "a female astronaut," "Bob Dylan," and similar silliness. Yesterday, someone wrote, "Forget feminism, you have to do a male or you'll leave out a whole chromosome!" What the writer meant was the Y chromosome, unique to males. If we sequenced a female, we wouldn't have the Y chromosome in our human sequence information.

Lee's footsteps resumed, and I returned to my transgenic mice, a project I was sharing with Carol Readhead. She was involved in a famous experiment that cured 'shaker' mice. The mice shook all the time and had a very short life span. The 'shaker' defect turned out to be a problem in wrapping their nerves with an insulator called myelin. Carol's team had injected the correct gene for myelin basic protein, and cured the mice. The cured mice were shown on the cover of Cell, one of the top scientific journals. Most people would say that Lee Hood cured the shaker mouse. It's hard for women scientists to get any credit.

At the time of my sabbatical, Lee had around one hundred people in his laboratory at Caltech. Most were postdoctoral fellows, but there were also a few students. I came to this laboratory to learn immunology because I had been studying rat and mouse aging, and interesting things happen to the immune system during aging. Occidental College was paying my salary, and I had an NIH grant, so Lee's laboratory only provided supplies for my study. Still, I was surprised when Lee actually agreed to let me come.

I believe he accepted me because of his brother, Myron Hood, a mathematician who was once on the Occidental College faculty. I knew Myron and Sue Hood well, because we had camped together all over California, but I thought what counted with Lee was our shared professional situation. Myron told his brother how hard it is at places where both teaching and research are expected. While at Oxy, Myron tried to do mathematical biology research only to find out his department lacked respect for 'applied mathematics'. So Lee felt that people like me deserved to be supported and helped to keep our hands in research.

I had Iwona for my assigned mentor that year. Before applying to come, I conferred with my friend Jane Sanders, who had moved there from Oxy, about which postdoctoral fellow to work with. I read the research descriptions in the Caltech annual report and selected ones I liked. Jane told me things like, "No, that one is very hard to get along with. This one is a tough person, but very intelligent. This one is nice, but the ideas are a bit far out." I selected Iwona, the 'tough person, but very intelligent' whose research interested me greatly, and asked to have her as a mentor for my research. She agreed, and we worked together amicably.

Iwona had an incredibly fast and penetrating intelligence, and she took on hard puzzles and worked through them with great elegance. Before coming to Caltech, she was a prime mover in the discovery of bacterial attenuation, a major regulatory process that is in all the textbooks. Just try to find her name with the experiment though. If anyone is credited, it is usually her · laboratory chief.

What perplexes me to this day is what drives wonderful women scientists to work as research associates for major portions of their careers rather than head their own groups. She was an example of this trend, and I saw many more while on this sabbatical. I didn't have a gut level understanding of them because I crave independence. I learned to generate interesting research ideas and wanted to have my own group to work on them and 'make scientific progress.' At that time I thought Iwona didn't crave independence, nor did it seem to me that she cared who got credit for her progress, although she has told me recently that she always did care who got credit. She definitely wanted to be on the cutting edge. It was far easier to be on the cutting edge in Lee Hood's group than to begin a new group and still be on that cutting edge.

I did understand the attractiveness of these positions in one way: it was an addictive connection to the scientific grapevine. I heard and learned so much during my year in Lee Hood's laboratory, as a Hoodlum as we called ourselves, it would take me several more years back at Oxy to sort it all out. We Hoodlums were at a node on the world information highway. If a laboratory in Finland discovered a new way to make a transgenic mouse or a new way antibody genes can diversify, we heard it the next day. Discussion focused on what the next breakthrough would be, and how to design a fast and convincing experiment to arrive at a new level of understanding.

My sabbatical year came to an end, and with it, my work in immunology. Late in the year, Iwona had a big party for the whole huge Hood group. Mike and I went and really enjoyed ourselves. Mike still talks about the thrill of hearing the famous Lee Hood play the recorder along with the folk guitarists who were singing there.

During the year I found myself slowly drowning in a sea of specialized terminology about the immune system, not to say jargon. So I jettisoned immunity as a focus, but continued my study of the molecular biology of aging, keeping my eyes open for connections to genomics. Later I got involved with Malcolm Campbell and the Genome Consortium for Active Teaching, a group helping professors who work with undergraduates to get to the cutting edge of genomics.

I continued to collaborate with Iwona for a time. Eventually, she moved to Texas with her husband, a physicist, and looked for a faculty position. University of Texas Southwestern Medical Center hired her as an Associate Professor but dangled the carrot of tenure for three years. At last she was given tenure. Such a position is the academic holy grail; if you get tenure, your position is funded by hard money and even if you're between grant funds, you still have a paying job. When I went on this sabbatical leave to Caltech, I already had tenure at Oxy.

But these women didn't want my kind of job. Like Barbara McClintock, the Nobel laureate in genetics described by biographer Evelyn Fox-Keller in A Feeling for the Organism, they want to be at research-intensive universities, not liberal arts colleges with a lot of teaching responsibilities.

Now I think back to my talk at the senior center, to "shooting the moon" with my predictions about the possibilities of genomics. Just a few years after my sabbatical, Leroy Hood and his group, including my friend Jane Sanders, invented a spectacular, new, cheaper, and more reliable way to find the DNA sequence of a gene, by using a different color of fluorescent dye to mark each of DNA's four different components. Today, sequencing individual human genomes is even cheaper, and it's predicted that a new technique may cut the price by 50-60%. Some are predicting an individual genome can be sequenced for $1000 by 2015. Individual medicine appears to be right around the corner. So I wasn't exaggerating to the seniors.

Individualized genome analysis for some genetic disorders is already available. It's possible to have one cell of an early embryo diagnosed and decide whether or not to implant the embryo based on the results. Women with breast cancer are sent for chemotherapy or not based on genomic analysis of which genes their tumors express. In 2009, a drug treatment recommendation for African-Americans only, based on genomics analysis, was released by the FDA. Individual drug treatment recommendations based on genomics don't seem far in the future any more. Today it is seems more likely that I was under-representing the real effects the project is having. Lee *is* shooting the moon, and it looks like he's going to make it.

CHAPTER 24
WHO AM I REALLY?

Before I began this memoir, I thought my goal, back in 1962 when I decided I wanted to study biochemical genetics, was to become that guy in the white coat and glasses with the beard, a professor at a major research university who wins the Nobel Prize for his important discovery. I didn't consider that I have no Y chromosome, so the "he" and the beard were out from the start. Lawrence Summers, the president of Harvard University got into trouble with his faculty in 2005 by saying that there are so few women scientists at Harvard because women don't have the dedication to work 80 hour weeks, and even if they do, there aren't as many women as men who are intrinsically good at science. He resigned and Derek Bok took over as President Pro Tem in summer, 2006.

But was Summers coming up with this idea out of left field? Unfortunately, he was not. At Harvard and other major research universities, after decades of attempting to increase the number of women faculty in science, they are still a tiny presence, less than ten percent of the faculty. MIT announced in spring, 2006 that its numbers of women in the science professoriate have reached a plateau at about 14%, after a sharp increase from 8% following Nancy Hopkins' report in 1999 on the status of MIT women science faculty. The liberal arts colleges are only a little better at hiring and keeping women scientists. At Pomona College in 2006, the biology department was almost half women, mathematics is about a third, and physics, chemistry, and geology each had one woman on permanent faculty.

In writing this memoir and trying to answer Summers for my own satisfaction, I began to assess the fates of the women and men whom I knew at Yale in graduate school. They were all promising scientists at the time or they wouldn't have been admitted to the Yale graduate program in Biology. I could easily recall 11 women and 14 men from those classes; evidently the women made a stronger impression on me since there were more men as women each year. Of the women I recall, three are now at research universities, but only two of the three (18%) are professors. Of the men I recall, nine (64%) are now professors at research universities. Things have been tough for women who want to become a research university professor in science. As I mentioned, women who received the PhD in my day were directed to postdoctoral fellowships, and some remained research associates for the entirety of their careers.

In terms of getting research university positions, the situation for women improved after my Yale entry class. In a sense, my class fell between the pre-Betty Friedan Eisenhower-era stay-at-home women and the later time when the men of science were more prepared to have women join in. Sputnik had called, but no one was really prepared for us women to answer yet. However, two women that I knew from later Yale graduate school classes, Susan Gerbi and Mary Lou Pardue from Joe Gall's laboratory, are professors at Brown and MIT and have done well in research. Mary Lou was elected to the National Academy of Sciences based partly on her graduate work. She invented a way to locate a specific sequence of DNA within a cell by a method she called *in situ* hybridization. Many others of Joe Gall's students succeeded, to the point where he received an award for mentoring women scientists.

Looking back at my career, I'm saddened by the lack of community in many of my science interactions, while I look back on my personal life with a generally upbeat perspective. Science is an ongoing conversation. One of my most painful realizations over time has been the extent to which I'm not a very loud voice in that conversation. My papers are published, and I look over and over at the PubMed web site to see whether they have been cited by anyone else. Often enough, only my coauthors cite them. The role of methylation changes in aging is a new hot topic, but almost none of the current papers cite my earlier work founding the field.

Looking at the science aspect of my career, I'm still in love with DNA, and I still contribute to understanding how it is involved in the aging process. But I feel the lack of scientific camaraderie. I've made mistakes, but the cost in connections with other scientists has been beyond what anyone could reasonably have predicted from what I did. Men have made the kind of mistakes I've made and not been disconnected from scientific friendship. The "old boy network' is still going strong and at least some of the old girls seem to be disconnected from it. As my computer says to me all too frequently, "the network connection is not available at this time." The cost is one I share with many silent women of science, working quietly in hopes that their voices may someday be heard abroad in the land. I wish I had a wand to wave and make it so. I hope to find that my students are connected to a strong scientific network when they are professors.

I am glad today that I'm not a Harvard professor, but I still have questions about how I arrived here at Pomona College. Did I end up here and not at Harvard because of fate, chance, or choice? Summers would be right if there was no way I or any of my female colleagues could have won the Nobel Prize and been hired at Harvard because our neurons were wired wrong for science. I find that explanation unsatisfying, since I almost always got kudos for my scientific understanding and creativity until I finished Yale.

Why did I fall off course to achieve my original goals? I could certainly point to lacks in mentoring, to deficient community and mutual support among scientists, and to some outright prejudice as possible causes of my failure to achieve my original image.

On the other hand, writing this memoir brought my time with Young and Borek and at Occidental College into better focus. I came to understand that I had passed "an invisible boundary" as Thoreau once said, and that I put aside that Nobel laureate/Harvard professor dream so that "new, universal, and more liberal laws" began to encompass me. I chose for human connections, for family, children, and students, when a more classical scientist would have put those features of life on hold and totally immersed herself in science. I continue to feel that a woman in science should not need to reject family life and teaching to succeed in discovering interesting and important new findings. She should be able to "have it all," not in the material sense but in the sense of fulfilling her potentials.

As Nobel laureate Cristiane Nusslein-Volhard said in a recent interview with Claudia Dreifus of the *New York Times*, "...there is a problem to combine family with a scientific profession. Because the profession is really more than full time—and requires a lot of energy." I have no regrets about my choices, but if I had chosen to be a workaholic scientist, I'm almost certain I would have been bursting with regrets at missing the opportunity for family and student connections. Having made a choice for family and students doesn't imply that I'm any the less passionate about my science, but it probably explains why my discovery rate has been slower than that of my male colleagues from way back when.

I was interested to read in the *Yale Alumni Magazine* for March/April, 2006 that only 18.7% of the Arts and Sciences faculty at Yale today are women. The title of the article by Nadia Labi asked," Do changing diapers and helping with homework leave time for world-class scholarship?" She reported that 88% of surveyed junior women faculty members felt "their child care responsibilities had definitely or somewhat affected their tenure prospects at Yale." A similar point was made in March, 2006 in *Nature Biotechnology*, in an article entitled "Missing: entrepreneurial women in biotech." That article cites Maria Pitone of the Wharton School's comment, "Research shows that women get to a certain point in the organization and then they opt out." They opt out when they must choose between promotion and motherhood, a choice that I, too made in the motherhood direction.

Today, I question whether science should demand the utmost in dedication from its devotees. There was a consensus for such an approach when I was learning science, but I hoped that it had been replaced by an understanding that human relationships had an important role in the life of a scientist. However, my friend Gail's daughter who recently completed graduate work at UCSF, has encountered almost exactly the same demands and expectations that I recall from that period of my own life. I would rather have found that now even men are taking parental leaves, that working 16-hour days isn't expected any more, and that average citizens no longer need to tell the typical scientist to "get a life!"

I'm interested in whether or not the Sputnik recruiting, and later efforts to broaden the access to science, have started to change the way science is done. Although there hasn't yet been a break in the demand for excessive dedication, I anticipate that one might happen in the future. The most encouraging sign to me is the demand for child care releases by young male professors. But another interesting aspect of this question is whether women focus on different aspects or approaches and add richness to the ways of doing science. Evelyn Fox-Keller back in 1996, in *Reflections on Gender and Science*, wrote that both the types of problems and the approaches could be different for women than for men.

One of my CUR friends, Jan Serie from Macalester College,

once told me that she thought women in science might be more integrative, more holistic, and have more of an overview of the connections between parts. I consider this a reasonable summary, and like most capsule views, it isn't accurate in every case, but it may summarize a trend. It might be that saying women like "holistic science," with its tones of alternative medicine, sounds like I'm taking women's science lightly, but I'm not. I hope the examples I have in mind will give you a clearer picture of what I mean. First, there is Mary Lou Pardue, student at Yale after my time and now an MIT professor. Some of her research focused on small, linear problems such as the mechanism of heat shock response. But other parts of it asked about huge issues with enormous detail, such as which exact proteins, of hundreds possible, were involved in the protein packaging of along every chromosome in the genome. This global approach could reveal that adjacent genes tend to have the same sets of proteins bound, or that they never do. A lot about how genes are regulated could be inferred from this study, but I've heard male scientists say it was too altruistic and didn't repay the amount of effort with enough publications to make it worthwhile. When she was at UCSF, Erin O'Shea did a similar catalog of where every non-essential protein in yeast occurred within the cell, painstakingly tagging every one with yellow fluorescent protein. Helpful to her, but also quite global and altruistic.

At times, I think I fit this holistic model. When my lab had first discovered that DNA methylation was decreased in aging mouse liver, I really wanted to examine sequences from every class of repeated DNA (unique, middle repetitive, and highly repetitive) to see if the change affected all of them equally. The year we planned those experiments, I argued about this survey of types of DNA with a couple of smart graduate students who came to visit our poster at the Gerontological Society. Both men thought I should pick ONE sequence and understand every jot and tittle of its demethylation and all of the regulatory implications of that one system. I couldn't be persuaded by these guys, although that was the classic pattern of linear science.

I tentatively conclude that overviews are more comfortable to female scientists. The overview could either be chosen as the first approach, or after many tiny, focused experiments are done, a synthesis could be attempted. I would argue that the focused experiments with a later synthesis is more of a male approach. If I'm right, then the choices of men versus women of which experiments to do first might only affect the order in which the puzzle pieces of scientific knowledge are accumulated. I think more exceptions could be discovered and understood early using a global approach, though. That could lead to faster progress overall.

If women do tend to gravitate towards the big picture, that preference for connecting all the dots may relate to their need to connect on a human level as well. Personally, I revel in connections, between molecules, between ideas, and between people, and maybe that's typical of women.

One more possibly feminine emphasis is cooperation rather than competition. Alice Wexler's book *Mapping Fate*, describing her sister Nancy's collaborative approach to achieving cloning of the gene for Huntington Disease, shows that way of working very clearly. It's interesting that the main proponent of the fusion of different organisms to form eukaryotic cells, sort of an ultimate in cooperation, has been a woman, Lynn Margulies. The different approaches to scientific problems by male versus female scientists could be complementary, if permitted to be so, creating a whole exceeding its parts.

After the period of this memoir, during my stint in administration, I was forced into reflection by breast cancer, I woke up to the fact that DNA hadn't been and wasn't my only love. I also loved introducing undergraduate students to research and doing things with my family. I had to return to the faculty to restore the parts of my life that nourished me. As a dean, my life seemed to withdraw my resources without replenishing them. By this time, I wasn't thinking about research universities at all, but I still loved doing science and wanted to get my laboratory started again after a five-year lapse during my academic Vice Presidency. With a year of training supported by an NSF POWRE grant for women returning to science, I was able to get both an NSF grant and later also an NIH grant to get my laboratory rolling again.

Now my students and I are trying to figure out how the aging clock is reset. The investigation is rewarding, even if it only produces future scientists. I learned that from CUR, as a delayed insight from my rejection by NIH, and it was reinforced by my reflection as an administrator: I produce two products for science. One is new findings. One is future scientists. So simple, so satisfying. So what if I don't win the Nobel Prize?

Although I am quite sure I'm happier than I would ever have been as a Harvard Professor, I'd still like to tell former President Summers that I could have done it. If I had been accepted for graduate study at Princeton or Caltech. If Yale had mentored female PhD's into jobs at research universities. If I hadn't had to leave behind my research when I got married the first time. If I had been hired at UCR or UCLA instead of Occidental College. If I had been luckier when I chose the Error Catastrophe Hypothesis to test. If NSF and NIH hadn't acquired reviewers who agreed with Hamilton Smith, who said on the radio that only large and well funded groups can do science today.

But if those things had come to pass, then a lot of what I value in life wouldn't have happened. Now I'm a scientist who values the close relationships with my family and also with undergraduates just finding science. I value my ability to choose original problems that I really like. I'm proud of how I worked with CUR colleagues to solve common problems. If I'd been hired at Harvard, I might never have married. I might have been an admirable, more-frequently-cited scientist like a brilliant woman student I taught at Oxy. For my own satisfaction as a person, I don't think I've been living a mistake. However, I must admit that when I read Summers' comments, I had an urge to shake him and tell him about my letter from Princeton graduate school and how hard it was for women compared to men to find research university positions after a Yale PhD was completed.

My life has been a "life in science for a woman", a woman who might have been the missing person on the Harvard faculty under different circumstances. I'm happy to be a married woman and mother, professor of biology at Pomona College with my bright and avid undergraduates. I did pass Thoreau's invisible boundary and find a more universal welcoming place. I found my life in balance. I can still follow the quiz-show- inspired image of a thread leading towards the golden door hiding secrets of DNA along with my students, while having many warm relationships.

ACKNOWLEDGEMENTS

I appreciate the help of many people in writing this book. First and foremost, my heartfelt thanks go to my husband Michael and my daughter Heather for support, love, and many helpful discussions and fast reviews for various purposes.

Second, thanks to my first readers, Katherine Hagedorn and Margaret Waller at Pomona College, for gentle guidance and encouragement when I thought I was about through but had barely started.

Third, I would like to recognize and thank my wonderful critique groups and support groups, Libby Grandy's critique group at Borders Montclair, Deb Martinson's Occidental Writers Network, Stephanie Montgomery's Memoir Café online group, the California Writers Club, Last Sunday Writers, Kathryn Wilkens' group, and other groups I have visited that have given me ideas.

Finally, I owe a debt to friends who agreed to read all or part of the manuscript for various purposes: Sterling Keeley at University of Hawaii, Johanna Hardin at Pomona College, and Meg Mathies at Scripps College who read it for amount and clarity of science content; Cecilia Fox at Occidental College, Phoebe Lostroh from Colorado College, my daughter Heather Hoopes, my administrative assistant Gail Sundberg, and a postdoctoral fellow, Nina Goodey who read it for continuity and highlights; and Mike Foley from Writer's Review and my friend the author Gayle

Greene for helping me to achieve a writing style with as much style, grace, and clarity as possible. I also deeply appreciate readers who tried to check my recollections of things. Where the writing is not on target, it is surely my fault and not theirs: Terry Krulwich, Ann Lacy, Helen Haberman, Chris Craney, Iwona Stroynowski, Peter Stanley, Betchen Barber, and Nalsey Tinberg.

I used a number of books to help me recall and contextualize events that happened during my life, and to examine how others have portrayed women's lives in science. I particularly recommend Evelyn Fox Keller's *A Feeling for the Organism*, Vivian Gornick's *Women in Science*, and Estzkowitz, Kemelgor and Uzzi's *Athena Unbound* for insights related to those I present.

ABOUT THE AUTHOR

Laura L. Mays Hoopes is Professor of Biology and Molecular Biology at Pomona College in Claremont, CA. She received the AB from Goucher College and the PhD from Yale University in biological sciences, a certificate in Creative Writing from UCLA and an MFA in Creative Writing from San Diego State University. Laura has published articles and short stories in *Christian Science Monitor*, *The Chaffin Journal*, *North Carolina Literary Review*, *The Fat City Review* and other venues. She is currently at work on two novels and several short stories, and she enjoys the freedom of fiction after the constraints of science writing. Laura resides with her husband in Claremont, CA, on the eastern fringe of Los Angeles County near the desert. For more information, visit www.lauralmayshoopes.com.

Made in the USA
Las Vegas, NV
29 October 2021